VOCABULARY WORKSHOP

LEVEL ORANGE

Jerome Shostak

Sadlier-Oxford
A Division of William H. Sadlier, Inc.
New York, NY 10005-1002

VOCABULARY WORKSHOP

The classic program for:

- developing and enriching vocabulary resources
- promoting more effective communication in today's world
- improving vocabulary skills assessed on standardized tests

Acknowledgments

Corbis Bettman: 19, 43; Macduff Everton: 25; Kevin R. Morris: 31; Peter Johnson: 77; George Hall: 83; David H. Wells: 89.

Stock Market/ Mugshots: 113.

Tony Stone Images/ Alan Thorton: 13; Mark Joseph: 107; Zigy Kaluzny: 119; Cosmo Condina: 125.

Illustrator

Daryl Stevens: 41, 71, 105, 135.

Copyright © 1999 by William H. Sadlier, Inc.

Request for permission to make copies of any part of this work should be mailed to:

Permissions Department
William H. Sadlier, Inc.
9 Pine Street
New York, NY 10005-1002

S is a registered trademark of William H. Sadlier, Inc.

Printed in the United States of America

ISBN: 0-8215-0404-5

9/04 03

CONTENTS

FOREWORD

For nearly half a century Vocabulary Workshop has proven a highly successful tool for promoting and guiding systematic vocabulary growth. Level Orange, one of two new additions to the Vocabulary Workshop series, is meant both to help younger students *increase* their vocabulary and to *improve* their vocabulary skills. It has also been designed to help prepare students for vocabulary-related items found in standardized tests.

Mastery of the words introduced in this text will make students better readers and better writers—better readers because they will be able to understand and appreciate more of what they read, and better writers because they will have at hand a greater pool of words with which to express themselves. Many of the words introduced in this book are ones that students will encounter in social studies, science, and literature, as well as in their reading outside the classroom.

Word List   Level Orange contains 192 basic words selected on the basis of currency in present-day usage, frequency in recognized vocabulary lists and on standardized tests, and the latest grade-placement research.

Units   The words are grouped in 16 short, stimulating units that include: definitions (with pronunciation and parts of speech), reinforcement of meanings, synonyms and antonyms, in-context sentence completions, and word-association exercises.

Reviews   Four Reviews (one for every four units) reinforce the work of the units with challenging exercises that include Analogies, Vocabulary in Context, and Word Games.

Two Cumulative Reviews, the first covering the first 8 units and the second covering the last 8 units, provide further reinforcement.

Assessment   The Diagnostic Test provides ready assessment of student needs and preparedness at the outset of the term.

The Final Mastery Test provides end-of-term assessment of student achievement.

Teacher Materials   A Teacher's Annotated Edition supplies answers to all of the exercises in the pupil text and an introduction to the Vocabulary Workshop program.

The Supplementary Testing Program provides separate testing exercises covering the material found in the pupil text. Answers are in the Teacher's Annotated Edition.

THE VOCABULARY OF VOCABULARY

English has a large group of special terms to describe how words are used and how they are related to one another. These terms make up what we might call the "vocabulary of vocabulary." Learning to understand and use the "vocabulary of vocabulary" will help you to get better results in your vocabulary-building program.

Part of Speech

Every word in English plays some role in the language. What that role is determines how a word is classified grammatically. These classifications are called "parts of speech." In English there are eight parts of speech: nouns, pronouns, verbs, adjectives, adverbs, prepositions, conjunctions, and interjections. All of the words introduced in this book are nouns (abbreviated *n.*), verbs (*v.*), or adjectives (*adj.*).

A **noun** names a person, place, or thing. *Sister, lake,* and *glass* are nouns. So are *Jefferson, Miami,* and *Olympics.* Nouns also name things such as ideas and feelings; for example, *freedom* and *joy* are nouns.

Verbs express action or a state of being. *Bake, fetch, arrange, lose, hear, think, see, come, sing,* and *know* are verbs.

Adjectives describe or give information about nouns or other adjectives. *Large, red, soft, heavy, old, new, pretty, useful, stormy,* and *glad* are adjectives.

Many English words act as more than one part of speech. The word *light,* for example, can be a verb or a noun. Its part of speech depends upon the way it is used.

NOUN: We saw a *light* in one of the windows. [*light* names a thing]

VERB: I got up to *light* the candles. [*light* expresses an action]

EXERCISES   For each sentence circle the choice that identifies the part of speech of the word in **boldface.**

1. The president gave a **great** speech.
   - a. noun
   - b. verb
   - c. adjective

2. Why don't we **walk** to the store?
   - a. noun
   - b. verb
   - c. adjective

3. It will be a pleasant **walk**.
   - a. noun
   - b. verb
   - c. adjective

4. They slept through the **boring** movie.
   - a. noun
   - b. verb
   - c. adjective

5. He held on with one **hand**.
   - a. noun
   - b. verb
   - c. adjective

6. Please **hand** me the scissors.
   - a. noun
   - b. verb
   - c. adjective

Synonyms and Antonyms

Synonyms

A **synonym** is a word that means *the same* or *nearly the same* as another word.

EXAMPLES   smile — grin   easy — simple

go — leave   scare — frighten

rich — wealthy   heat — warmth

EXERCISES   For each of the following groups circle the choice that is most nearly the **same** in meaning as the word in **boldface**.

1. **rescue**	2. **car**	3. **run**	4. **loud**
a. forget	a. automobile	a. step	a. dull
b. save	b. moped	b. stare	b. sharp
c. pretend	c. aircraft	c. find	c. noisy
d. hurry	d. carriage	d. dash	d. soft

Antonyms

An **antonym** is a word that is *opposite* or *nearly opposite* in meaning to another word.

EXAMPLES   high — low   win — lose

shout — whisper   pleasure — pain

war — peace   happy — sad

EXERCISES   For each of the following groups circle the choice that is most nearly **opposite** in meaning to the word in **boldface**.

1. **forget**	2. **buy**	3. **first**	4. **strength**
a. lose	a. ask	a. big	a. courage
b. remember	b. watch	b. small	b. noise
c. tell	c. sell	c. best	c. bravery
d. write	d. take	d. last	d. weakness

Context Clues

When you turn to the "Completing the Sentence" and "Vocabulary in Context" exercises in this book, look for clues built into the passages to guide you to the correct answers. There are three basic types of clues.

Restatement Clues   A restatement clue gives a *definition of*, or a *synonym for*, a missing word.

EXAMPLE   The long walk through the <u>cold</u> rain left me wet and
_____.

a. thrilled   b. afraid   c. happy   d. chilled

Contrast Clues   A contrast clue gives an *antonym for*, or a phrase meaning *the opposite of*, a missing word.

EXAMPLE   Because we did not get to the airport <u>on time</u>, we were
_____ for our flight.

a. late   b. early   c. sleepy   d. ready

Situational Clues   Sometimes the situation itself, as it is outlined in the sentence or passage, suggests the word that is missing but does not state the meaning directly.

EXAMPLE   If you want to wear that <u>torn</u> jacket again, you will have to
_____ it first.

a. buy   b. wash   c. mend   d. iron

To figure out which word is missing from the sentence, ask yourself this question: What would you have to do before you could wear a "torn" jacket again? Would you buy it? wash it? mend it? iron it?

EXERCISES   Use context clues to choose the word that best completes each of the following sentences.

1. To take good _____ of your vegetable garden, you should water it and pull out the weeds.
   a. care   b. pictures   c. advantage   d. samples

2. After a week of heavy rain and strong winds, we welcomed the return to _____ and sunny weather.
   a. cloudy   b. calm   c. scary   d. foggy

3. To _____ for a test, you should review the lessons in your book and study your class notes.
   a. ask   b. read   c. write   d. prepare

Analogies

An **analogy** is a comparison. For example, we can make an analogy, or comparison, between a computer and a human brain.

In this book and in many standardized tests you will be asked to find the relationship between two words. Then, to show that you understand that relationship, you will be asked to choose another pair of words that show the same relationship.

EXAMPLES

1. **light** is to **dark** as
   a. sad is to unhappy
   b. windy is to breezy
   c. cold is to hot
   d. wet is to damp

2. **eat** is to **dine** as
   a. stand is to sit
   b. cry is to weep
   c. mend is to tear
   d. run is to walk

In the first example, note that *light* and *dark* are **antonyms**; they are opposite in meaning. Of the four choices given, which pair is made up of words that are also antonyms, or opposite in meaning? The answer, of course, is *c, cold is to hot*.

In the second example, note that *eat* and *dine* are **synonyms**; they have nearly the same meaning. Of the four choices given, which pair is made up of words that are also synonyms, or have nearly the same meaning? The answer is *b, cry is to weep*.

There are many other kinds of analogies besides ones based on synonyms and antonyms. For each of the exercises that follow, first study carefully the pair of words in **boldface**. Then, when you have figured out the relationship between the two words, look for another pair that has the same relationship. Circle the item that best completes the analogy, and then write the relationship on the lines provided.

3. **tulip** is to **flower** as
   a. apple is to fruit
   b. chalk is to crayon
   c. wood is to table
   d. bird is to crow

4. **bat** is to **baseball** as
   a. field is to soccer
   b. coach is to team
   c. ticket is to game
   d. stick is to hockey

5. **hat** is to **head** as
   a. scarf is to gloves
   b. wool is to sweater
   c. shoe is to foot
   d. sleeve is to shirt

Relationship: _____

_____

_____

_____

Relationship: _____

_____

_____

_____

Relationship: _____

_____

_____

_____

PRONUNCIATION KEY

The pronunciation is given for every basic word introduced in this book. The symbols, which are shown below, are similar to those that appear in most standard dictionaries. The author has consulted a large number of dictionaries for this purpose but has relied primarily on *Webster's Third New International Dictionary* and *The Random House Dictionary of the English Language (Unabridged)*.

Of course there are many English words, including some that appear in this book, for which two (or more) pronunciations are commonly accepted. In virtually all cases where such words occur in this book, students are given just one pronunciation. Exceptions to this rule are made, however, in cases when the pronunciation of a word changes according to its part of speech. For example, as a noun the word *object* is pronounced 'äb jekt; as a verb it is pronounced əb 'jekt. It is believed that these relatively simple pronunciation guides will be readily usable by students. It should be emphasized, however, that the best way to learn the pronunciation of a word is to listen to and imitate an educated speaker.

Vowels	ā	lake	e	stress	ü	boot, new
	a	mat	ī	knife	u̇	foot, pull
	â	care	i	sit	ə	rug, broken
	ä	bark, bottle	ō	flow	ər	bird, better
	au̇	doubt	ô	all, cord		
	ē	beat, wordy	oi	oil		

Consonants	ch	child, lecture	s	cellar	wh	what
	g	give	sh	shun	y	yell
	j	gentle, bridge	th	thank	z	is
	ŋ	sing	t̶h̶	those	zh	measure

All other consonants are sounded as in the alphabet.

Stress	The accent mark *precedes* the syllable receiving the major stress: en 'rich

Diagnostic Test

For each of the following items circle the letter for the word or phrase that best expresses the meaning of the word in **boldface** in the introductory phrase.

Example
asked for a **hint**
a. job   (b.) clue   c. napkin   d. book

1. **thaw** the frozen fields
   a. plow   b. warm   c. cross   d. graze

2. follow our **policy**
   a. guidelines   b. clues   c. instincts   d. leaders

3. **oppose** the decision
   a. agree with   b. wait for   c. listen to   d. fight against

4. write an **outstanding** composition
   a. long   b. short   c. good   d. excellent

5. **scamper** on the grass
   a. run around   b. sit still   c. lie down   d. drink tea

6. a **coarse** washcloth
   a. clean   b. old   c. worn   d. rough

7. pick up my **baggage**
   a. wrappers   b. lunch trays   c. suitcases   d. clothes

8. **trudge** to school
   a. skip happily   b. ride swiftly   c. walk slowly   d. drive carefully

9. a **noticeable** dent in the car
   a. tiny   b. visible   c. new   d. old

10. **drench** our clothes
    a. find   b. deliver   c. stain   d. soak

11. **merit** a reward
    a. return   b. receive   c. earn   d. present

12. the **babble** of the brook
    a. length   b. gurgle   c. color   d. current

13. **survive** the shipwreck
    a. hear about   b. hope for   c. swim by   d. live through

14. began to feel **drowsy**
    a. sleepy   b. sad   c. angry   d. happy.

15. **adorn** with sparkling jewels
    a. spoil   b. decorate   c. ruin   d. leave

16. seemed to be **uneasy**
    a. tired   b. relaxed   c. thoughtful   d. embarrassed

17. **offend** the whole audience
    a. please   b. anger   c. fear   d. delight

18. the **essential** ingredient
    a. expensive   b. delicious   c. rare   d. main

19. **grasp** the bike's handlebars
    a. paint   b. remove   c. break   d. grab

20. known for their **noble** deeds
    a. many   b. wicked   c. remarkable   d. selfish

21. **elevate** your broken foot
    a. raise   b. bandage   c. heal   d. forget

22. **stun** the onlookers
    a. amuse   b. shock   c. praise   d. watch

23. gave an honest **response**
    a. answer   b. try   c. excuse   d. story

24. the **annual** school picnic
    a. indoor   b. important   c. yearly   d. outdoor

25. heard the **clatter** in the kitchen
    a. clanking   b. dripping   c. laughter   d. speech

Definitions

Study the spelling, pronunciation, part of speech, and definition given for each of the words below. Write the word in the blank space in the sentence that follows. Then read the synonyms and antonyms.

1. **celebrity**
(sə 'le brə tē)

(n.) a well-known person; someone who is famous; fame
Her popular paintings have made her a _____ in the art world.
SYNONYMS: a star; fame
ANTONYMS: an unknown, nobody; anonymity

2. **counsel**
('kaůn səl)

(n.) opinions or ideas given for a plan of action; a talk that leads to a decision; a lawyer
The head of the law firm is serving as the lead _____ for this trial.
(v.) to give advice or an opinion; to offer help
After we lost a very close game, our coach tried to _____ us on how to accept defeat.
SYNONYMS: advice, wisdom, guidance; a lawyer; to help, advise, recommend

3. **demonstrate**
('dem ən strāt)

(v.) to clearly explain, show or prove with examples, models, or experiments; to gather in public to support an opinion or cause
To become a band member you must _____ some musical skill.
SYNONYMS: to show, model, prove, illustrate, reveal
ANTONYM: to hide

4. **drowsy**
('draů zē)

(adj.) ready to fall asleep, sleepy
After eating that big dinner, I felt too _____ to read.
SYNONYMS: sleepy, tired, sluggish
ANTONYMS: alert, wakeful

5. **essential**
(i 'sen chəl)

(adj.) of the highest importance, necessary
Food, water, and shelter are _____ to survival.
(n.) something necessary or very important
When you pack for a long trip, start with the _____.
SYNONYMS: necessary, vital, key, basic
ANTONYMS: unimportant, minor, unnecessary

6. **hardship**
('härd ship)

(n.) something that causes suffering or difficulty; a condition that is hard to bear
The pioneers had to live with many a _____.
SYNONYMS: a burden, ordeal, misfortune
ANTONYM: ease, comfort

Tractor-trailer rigs **haul** (word 7) goods over the nation's interstate highway system.

7. **haul**
   (hôl)

(v.) to move by pulling, dragging, or carting, sometimes in a vehicle; to apply force to transport something

A truck came to _____ away the trash.

(n.) the amount taken or won at one time

The boat brought in a good _____ of fish.

SYNONYMS: to lug, pull, cart, drag, carry, lift, tug; a yield, catch

8. **humble**
   ('həm bəl)

(adj.) low in rank or position; plain, not proud or grand

The family lived in a _____ cottage.

(v.) to take away one's spirit, power, fame, or independence

What will it take to _____ the proud king?

SYNONYMS: modest, simple, plain, earthy; to shame, embarrass
ANTONYMS: bold, grand; to empower, raise up

9. **pledge**
   (plej)

(n.) something given as a sign of a promise, especially money meant for a good cause; a sign or promise to fulfill an agreement

We can give a _____ of ten dollars to the fund.

(v.) to promise

A bride and groom _____ to honor each other.

SYNONYMS: a promise, guarantee; to vow, swear, vouch

10. **sincere**
    (sin 'sēr)

(adj.) without pretending; with honesty and real feeling

They offered a _____ apology.

SYNONYMS: genuine, true, heartfelt
ANTONYMS: false, phony

11. **stampede**
    (stam 'pēd)

(n.) a wild rush of animals or people, usually when frightened

The flood forced a _____ of cattle to higher ground.

(v.) to run away or cause to scatter in a wild manner, often in panic; to rush forward together as a crowd

The fans began to _____ toward the stage.

SYNONYMS: a flight, rush, dash; to bolt, charge, panic
ANTONYMS: to stroll, wander

12. **suitable**
    ('sü tə bəl)

(adj.) just right or appropriate; well matched

I'm going shopping for a _____ outfit to wear.

SYNONYMS: appropriate, proper, fitting, right
ANTONYMS: inappropriate, mismatched, improper

Match the Meaning

For each item below choose the word whose meaning is suggested by the clue given. Then write the word in the space provided.

1. A forest fire made the frightened herd _____ toward the river.
   a. demonstrate   b. stampede   c. pledge   d. haul

2. To offer helpful advice is to give _____.
   a. counsel   b. haul   c. celebrity   d. pledge

3. Something that brings suffering is called a _____.
   a. hardship   b. celebrity   c. counsel   d. pledge

4. By 10 P.M., we were too tired and _____ to play chess.
   a. humble   b. sincere   c. drowsy   d. suitable

5. Bread is _____ for making sandwiches.
   a. humble   b. sincere   c. drowsy   d. essential

6. Watch carefully as I _____ how to make tacos.
   a. counsel   b. demonstrate   c. pledge   d. stampede

7. To give a promise is to make a _____.
   a. stampede   b. haul   c. pledge   d. hardship

8. Losing may _____ that boastful coach.
   a. demonstrate   b. haul   c. counsel   d. humble

9. One way to move a heavy box is to _____ it on a wagon.
   a. demonstrate   b. stampede   c. haul   d. pledge

10. People who mean what they say are _____.
    a. sincere   b. essential   c. drowsy   d. suitable

11. Famous people don't always enjoy their _____.
    a. pledge   b. stampede   c. hardship   d. celebrity

12. A(n) _____ gift is one that fits the occasion perfectly.
    a. humble   b. essential   c. suitable   d. drowsy

Synonyms

*For each item below choose the word that is most nearly the **same** in meaning as the word or phrase in **boldface**. Then write your choice on the line provided.*

1. thanked her for her **guidance**
   a. celebrity   b. pledge   c. counsel   d. stampede   _____

2. **promise** to repay the loan
   a. pledge   b. counsel   c. demonstrate d. haul   _____

3. **drag** the stuffed suitcase
   a. haul   b. counsel   c. pledge   d. stampede   _____

4. **modest** words of a simple prayer
   a. essential   b. suitable   c. drowsy   d. humble   _____

5. **showed** how to dive
   a. demonstrated b. stampeded c. pledged   d. hauled   _____

6. bring **appropriate** clothing
   a. humble   b. sincere   c. drowsy   d. suitable   _____

Antonyms

*For each item below choose the word that is most nearly **opposite** in meaning to the word or phrase in **boldface**. Then write your choice on the line provided.*

1. a life of **ease**
   a. counsel   b. pledge   c. stampede   d. hardship   _____

2. a **false** smile
   a. essential   b. drowsy   c. sincere   d. humble   _____

3. found an **unimportant** clue
   a. sincere   b. essential   c. humble   d. suitable   _____

4. **unknowns** in the crowd
   a. stampedes   b. counsels   c. hardships   d. celebrities   _____

5. was **alert** during the movie
   a. sincere   b. humble   c. drowsy   d. suitable   _____

6. **stroll** down the ramp
   a. demonstrate b. stampede   c. pledge   d. counsel   _____

Completing the Sentence

From the list of words on pages 12–13, choose the one that best completes each item below. Then write the word in the space provided. (You may have to change the word's ending.)

THE VISITING FOLKSINGER

■ We are excited that a real _____ is coming to visit our class. It's not very often that we have the chance to meet someone so famous.

■ "We want to welcome our guest warmly, but let's not _____ to the door. Someone might get hurt!" our teacher said.

■ Our visitor sings songs about his _____ hometown—the same modest little town where our teacher grew up.

■ The _____ they experienced then are hard for us to imagine today. Compared to the difficulties they faced, we have it pretty easy.

RIGHTS IN AMERICA

■ In America, one of our _____ freedoms is the right to free speech. Some people consider it our most important right.

■ Our laws allow people to _____ in public, even to support an unpopular cause.

■ People can get legal _____ if they believe their rights have been taken away.

■ It's up to the courts to decide if the complaints are _____ or phony. If a judge believes that a complaint is made up, he or she may throw it out.

MEDICAL RESEARCH

■ The scientists made a _____ to publish the results of their experiments fully and honestly.

■ They will study whether a new medicine is _____ for children. If it is found to be appropriate, the medicine should be in drug stores next year.

■ It's amazing how much equipment they _____ into the lab! It must have taken a big truck to deliver it all.

■ The scientists often work late, but they stop when they get too _____ to concentrate.

 *Circle the letter next to the word or expression that best completes the sentence or answers the question. Pay special attention to the word in **boldface**.*

1. Which of the following is probably a **celebrity**?
   a. a star baseball player
   b. a nurse
   c. a local plumber
   d. a florist

2. If you need **counsel**, you might
   a. take a nap
   b. walk the dog
   c. call a lawyer
   d. wash the dishes

3. We might see a **drowsy** person
   a. stretched out on the couch
   b. going jogging
   c. starting a difficult project
   d. hanging wallpaper

4. A **pledge** should be
   a. honest
   b. difficult
   c. funny
   d. false

5. To **haul** a pony, you would use a
   a. skateboard
   b. horse trailer
   c. backpack
   d. fire engine

6. A **suitable** item for the pool is
   a. a snowshoe
   b. a piano
   c. a towel
   d. toothpaste

7. A real **hardship** for a goldfish would be to have
   a. a boring fishbowl
   b. a purple fishbowl
   c. an empty fishbowl
   d. a square fishbowl

8. A **humble** person might say
   a. "I deserve more!"
   b. "I don't deserve it."
   c. "Show me the prize!"
   d. "I'm number one!"

9. An **essential** part of a parade is
   a. cotton candy
   b. a rainy day
   c. a marching band
   d. a bunch of roses

10. I can best **demonstrate** ballet
    a. in a phone booth
    b. on a stage
    c. in a shoe store
    d. on the radio

11. A **sincere** person would
    a. play a trick on you
    b. get you a present
    c. tell you the truth
    d. throw a party

12. Why might crowds **stampede**?
    a. They are tired.
    b. They are bored.
    c. They are curious.
    d. They are afraid.

Study the spelling, pronunciation, part of speech, and definition given for each of the words below. Write the word in the blank space in the sentence that follows. Then read the synonyms and antonyms.

1. **annual**
('an yü əl)

(adj.) coming each year; once a year; lasting a year
The _____ class picnic is planned for the last week of the school year.

(n.) a book or magazine that comes out once a year; a plant that lives or lasts for just one growing season
One of my poems will appear in the 1998 poetry _____.

SYNONYMS: yearly; a yearbook

2. **basic**
('bā sik)

(adj.) having to do with the main or starting point of something
We understand the _____ idea of the game.

(n., usually plural) a key element or part
I got the _____ of addition in first grade.

SYNONYMS: essential, key, primary, fundamental

3. **competition**
(käm pə 'ti shən)

(n.) trying to outdo others; a game or contest
I am planning to enter the kite-flying _____.

SYNONYMS: a contest, rivalry, match, test
ANTONYM: cooperation

4. **contract**
(*n.*, 'kän trakt;
v., kən 'trakt)

(n.) an agreement or understanding that can be enforced by law; a document that explains legal conditions
Many people who buy computers also buy a service _____.

(v.) to make or grow smaller; to come down with, as a sickness
Some soft woods _____ when they dry.

SYNONYMS: an agreement, arrangement, deal, pact; to shrink; to catch, get
ANTONYMS: to expand, enlarge

5. **dismiss**
(dis 'mis)

(v.) to send away or permit to leave; to remove from a job; to stop thinking about
Our teacher will not _____ the class until we are all quiet.

SYNONYMS: to reject, fire, drop, discharge
ANTONYMS: to hire, hold, consider, employ

6. **neglect**
(ni 'glekt)

(v.) to hold back care or attention; to fail to follow through
You won't do well in school if you _____ your homework.

(n.) a steady lack of care, often because of carelessness or laziness
Our rose garden suffers from _____.

SYNONYMS: to ignore, disregard, overlook, forget; inattention
ANTONYM: to pamper

Because they had to remain very still for long exposures, the subjects of early photographs often appear **stern** (word 11). Shown here is John Quincy Adams, the first President to be photographed.

7. **obtain**
(əb 'tān)

(v.) to get or gain through some effort
Customers can _____ rare coins in that shop.

SYNONYMS: to acquire, gather
ANTONYMS: to lose, forgo

8. **portion**
('pōr shən)

(n.) a section or piece; a part of the whole; a serving of food
I'll have a small _____ of soup.

SYNONYMS: a part, share, helping
ANTONYM: a whole

9. **recall**
(v., ri 'kôl;
n., 'rē kôl)

(v.) to bring back to mind; to remind one; to ask to return
Photographs help us _____ highlights of our trip.
(n.) the ability or act of remembering
He had no _____ at all of the story.

SYNONYMS: to remember, resemble; to revoke; a memory, recollection
ANTONYM: to forget

10. **sponsor**
('spän sər)

(n.) one who helps or takes responsibility for another person or group; a person or business that pays for an ad on radio or television
A generous _____ paid for new uniforms for everyone in the band.
(v.) to act as a sponsor to a group, person, or event
Many businesses _____ the Special Olympics.

SYNONYMS: a supporter, backer, provider; to support

11. **stern**
(stərn)

(adj.) not kindly or gentle; harsh-looking
The officer gave them a _____ warning.
(n.) the back end of a boat
You can climb the ladder in the _____.

SYNONYMS: harsh, sharp, severe, firm, strict, grim; the rear
ANTONYMS: gentle, tender, kindly; the bow

12. **vacant**
('vā kənt)

(adj.) not used, filled, or lived in; without thought or expression
This bus has no more _____ seats.

SYNONYMS: empty, unused, available, open; blank
ANTONYMS: full; occupied

Match the Meaning

For each item below choose the word whose meaning is suggested by the clue given. Then write the word in the space provided.

1. A weak memory leaves me with little or no _____.
   a. neglect   b. competition   c. recall   d. sponsor

2. The main point of a story is its _____ idea.
   a. annual   b. basic   c. stern   d. vacant

3. If you study hard, you will _____ a good grade.
   a. sponsor   b. obtain   c. dismiss   d. neglect

4. A _____ is a legal paper that people sign.
   a. sponsor   b. recall   c. competition   d. contract

5. Camping sites with no tents on them are _____.
   a. stern   b. vacant   c. annual   d. basic

6. If you _____ to water the flowers, they'll droop and die.
   a. neglect   b. dismiss   c. contract   d. recall

7. The Olympics is a _____ that attracts the world's best athletes.
   a. sponsor   b. contract   c. competition   d. portion

8. We can also call a part a _____.
   a. portion   b. contract   c. recall   d. competition

9. A once-a-year trip is a(n) _____ event.
   a. annual   b. basic   c. vacant   d. stern

10. To pay for a television show is to _____ it.
   a. sponsor   b. contract   c. recall   d. neglect

11. A person who is harsh and strict might be called _____.
   a. annual   b. vacant   c. basic   d. stern

12. If I _____ an idea, I stop thinking about it.
   a. obtain   b. contract   c. dismiss   d. recall

Synonyms

*For each item below choose the word that is most nearly the **same** in meaning as the word or phrase in **boldface**. Then write your choice on the line provided.*

1. **acquire** a set of paints
   a. recall   b. obtain   c. neglect   d. dismiss   _____

2. the **key** facts of their argument
   a. vacant   b. basic   c. stern   d. annual   _____

3. **fire** that careless truck driver
   a. dismiss   b. recall   c. neglect   d. portion   _____

4. my **share** of the reward
   a. portion   b. contract   c. recall   d. competition   _____

5. the high school **yearbook**
   a. contract   b. sponsor   c. annual   d. competition   _____

6. a **supporter** of the local dance company
   a. contract   b. sponsor   c. portion   d. neglect   _____

Antonyms

*For each item below choose the word that is most nearly **opposite** in meaning to the word or phrase in **boldface**. Then write your choice on the line provided.*

1. a **kindly** gaze
   a. vacant   b. basic   c. stern   d. annual   _____

2. **expand** its wings
   a. obtain   b. dismiss   c. recall   d. contract   _____

3. an **occupied** seat
   a. vacant   b. annual   c. basic   d. stern   _____

4. **forget** the words to the song
   a. dismiss   b. recall   c. obtain   d. neglect   _____

5. **cooperation** among players
   a. contract   b. competition   c. portion   d. neglect   _____

6. **pamper** my best friend
   a. sponsor   b. dismiss   c. neglect   d. recall   _____

 **Completing the Sentence**

From the list of words on pages 18–19, choose the one that best completes each item below. Then write the word in the space provided. (You may have to change the word's ending.)

THAT'S S-P-E-L-L-I-N-G . . .

■ The National Spelling Bee is a(n) _____ event that takes place each spring in Washington, D.C.

■ The Spelling Bee's _____ is a company that owns newspapers and television stations.

■ This nationwide _____ is open to students through eighth grade. Thousands of students enter the spelling contest. They study long and hard to prepare for the event.

■ Interested students can _____ an official booklet that gives the words they may be asked to spell.

A GREEN PROJECT

■ Neighbors came up with a good way to use a(n) _____ city lot on their block. The lot had been empty since a fire had destroyed the building that had stood there.

■ "Let's try to turn at least a(n) _____ of it into a community garden," they said, "even if it is only a small part."

■ They wrote up a(n) _____ between themselves and the city to let them use some of the space as long as they would do all the work.

■ At first, city officials wanted to _____ the idea. They rejected the plan because they thought it might cost too much money.

■ But when local businesses agreed to donate _____ equipment, such as shovels, rakes, and seeds, the plan was approved.

POLLUTION SOLUTION

■ Air quality in some parts of the country got so bad that the government issued _____ warnings and began to pass strong anti-pollution laws.

■ The government threatened to force manufacturers to _____ cars and other machines that added too much pollution to the air. Most companies tried to make their products run more cleanly.

■ But companies that chose to _____ the warnings had to pay large fines for ignoring the new laws.

*Circle the letter next to the word or expression that best completes the sentence or answers the question. Pay special attention to the word in **boldface**.*

1. Which is *not* an **annual** event?
   a. your birthday
   b. the Fourth of July
   c. Thanksgiving
   d. the Winter Olympics

2. Before a big **competition**, you
   a. should practice or study
   b. should arrive an hour late
   c. should start a scrapbook
   d. should take a vacation

3. You might **dismiss** a pet-sitter
   a. who sang silly songs
   b. who fed the pets
   c. who ignored the pets
   d. who made a telephone call

4. Which is *not* a **basic** need?
   a. food
   b. music
   c. shelter
   d. clothing

5. Which might you **contract**?
   a. a dog house
   b. the chicken pox
   c. a pony ride
   d. a wild goose chase

6. One way to **obtain** a fossil is to
   a. buy one at a museum shop
   b. draw one in your notebook
   c. read about one in a book
   d. write a letter to the mayor

7. Workers who **neglect** their jobs
   a. might get fired
   b. might earn raises
   c. might win promotions
   d. might receive gifts

8. A fair **portion** of a shared lunch
   a. is a bite of a cookie
   b. is half of a sandwich
   c. is all the chocolate pudding
   d. is a spoonful of yogurt

9. We **recall** the party when we see
   a. a bowl of oatmeal
   b. a math test
   c. a bunch of balloons
   d. a rocket launch

10. A **sponsor** might be willing to
    a. give you a job
    b. learn your favorite dance
    c. borrow money from you
    d. listen to your radio

11. Where is the **stern** of a ship?
    a. at the front
    b. at the back
    c. at the side
    d. at the center

12. A **vacant** apartment has
    a. no air conditioning
    b. nobody living in it
    c. roomy closets
    d. very expensive rent

Definitions

Study the spelling, pronunciation, part of speech, and definition given for each of the words below. Write the word in the blank space in the sentence that follows. Then read the synonyms and antonyms.

1. **attractive**
(ə 'trak tiv)

(adj.) pleasing to the eye, mind, or senses; having the power to draw attention

Most people notice someone with an _____ smile.

SYNONYMS: appealing, likable, charming, beautiful, inviting
ANTONYMS: unappealing, unpleasant, disagreeable, offensive

2. **burden**
('bər dən)

(n.) something that is carried, a load; something that is very hard to bear

It is a _____ to keep a secret.

(v.) to weigh down or put too heavy a load on

I am sorry to _____ you with all of these heavy packages.

SYNONYMS: a weight, baggage, difficulty, hardship, worry; to load, afflict, oppress
ANTONYMS: a relief; to relieve, lighten

3. **consent**
(kən 'sent)

(v.) to agree to or approve; to give permission

My parents would not _____ to my staying up late.

(n.) approval or permission

The teacher needs our parents' _____ so that we can go on the class trip.

SYNONYMS: to allow, permit, accept; agreement, authorization
ANTONYMS: to disapprove, refuse, deny, disallow; refusal, denial

4. **dependable**
(di 'pen də bəl)

(adj.) capable of being relied on; trustworthy

A taxi driver needs a _____ car that always starts, even in bad weather.

SYNONYMS: trustworthy, reliable, responsible
ANTONYMS: unreliable, undependable, untrustworthy

5. **indicate**
('in də kāt)

(v.) to point to or point out; to be a sign of; to state or express briefly

The nurse told me that a skin rash may _____ an allergy or an insect bite.

SYNONYMS: to mark, show, signify, suggest, announce
ANTONYM: to conceal

6. **previous**
('prē vē əs)

(adj.) coming before in time or order

Our teacher asked us to please turn back to the _____ page.

SYNONYMS: earlier, preceding, prior, past
ANTONYMS: following, later, succeeding

Because they are often used to carry heavy loads, mules are sometimes called "beasts of **burden**" (word 2).

7. **qualify**
('kwä lə fī)

(v.) to be or become fit for something; to limit or narrow the meaning of
You must be eighteen years old to _____ to vote in a national election.

SYNONYMS: to authorize, entitle, prepare, suit; to limit, modify

8. **response**
(ri 'späns)

(n.) a reply or answer; a reaction to something
I am still waiting for a _____ to my letter.

SYNONYMS: an answer, acknowledgement, reaction

9. **shabby**
('sha bē)

(adj.) worn or faded from use or wear; dressed in worn-out clothes; not fair or generous
The child shivered in the _____ old coat.

SYNONYMS: ragged, run-down; mean, wretched; unkind
ANTONYMS: elegant, grand; lavish; generous, kind

10. **thaw**
(thô)

(v.) to melt or cause to melt; to warm up gradually
Let the turkey _____ in the refrigerator before you cook it.

(n.) a period of weather warm enough to melt ice and snow
We had an early _____ in January.

SYNONYMS: to melt, liquefy
ANTONYMS: to freeze, solidify

11. **urgent**
('ər jənt)

(adj.) needing or demanding immediate action or attention
The fire department answered an _____ call for help.

SYNONYMS: critical, pressing, immediate
ANTONYMS: unimportant, minor

12. **vanity**
('va nə tē)

(n.) the quality of being stuck-up or vain; having too much pride in one's looks or abilities; a dressing table
A person's display of _____ can be very annoying.

SYNONYMS: conceit, arrogance, pride
ANTONYMS: modesty, humility

Match the Meaning

For each item below, choose the word whose meaning is suggested by the clue given. Then write the word in the space provided.

1. The day before this one was the _____ day.
   a. previous   b. urgent   c. dependable   d. shabby

2. A heavy responsibility can be a _____.
   a. consent   b. burden   c. response   d. vanity

3. Our class got the principal's _____ to start a recycling project.
   a. thaw   b. burden   c. consent   d. vanity

4. Ice will _____ when the temperature gets above the freezing point.
   a. thaw   b. consent   c. qualify   d. indicate

5. Signs on highways _____ where the exits are.
   a. thaw   b. qualify   c. indicate   d. consent

6. You can always count on _____ people.
   a. urgent   b. shabby   c. attractive   d. dependable

7. You must be sixteen to _____ for a driver's license.
   a. thaw   b. burden   c. indicate   d. qualify

8. Too much pride in your own looks or abilities is _____.
   a. response   b. vanity   c. burden   d. consent

9. A faded and torn chair could be described as _____.
   a. previous   b. dependable   c. shabby   d. attractive

10. _____ window displays will draw the attention of shoppers.
    a. Attractive   b. Shabby   c. Urgent   d. Dependable

11. An _____ problem calls for quick action.
    a. attractive   b. previous   c. shabby   d. urgent

12. When someone asks you a question, you should give a _____.
    a. response   b. vanity   c. burden   d. thaw

Synonyms

*For each item below choose the word that is most nearly the **same** in meaning as the word or phrase in **boldface**. Then write your choice on the line provided.*

1. the beggar's **ragged** clothing
   a. previous   b. dependable   c. shabby   d. attractive   _____

2. the **pressure** of many responsibilities
   a. vanity   b. burden   c. response   d. thaw   _____

3. an **appealing** display of flowers
   a. dependable   b. shabby   c. attractive   d. urgent   _____

4. **certified** to fly an airplane
   a. thawed   b. burdened   c. qualified   d. indicated   _____

5. received an **answer** to my letter
   a. response   b. burden   c. vanity   d. consent   _____

6. our **agreement** to host the party
   a. response   b. thaw   c. vanity   d. consent   _____

Antonyms

*For each item below choose the word that is most nearly **opposite** in meaning to the word or phrase in **boldface**. Then write your choice on the line provided.*

1. an **unimportant** message
   a. previous   b. dependable   c. urgent   d. attractive   _____

2. **unreliable** information
   a. previous   b. urgent   c. shabby   d. dependable   _____

3. the **following** question
   a. urgent   b. attractive   c. previous   d. shabby   _____

4. began to **freeze**
   a. indicate   b. qualify   c. consent   d. thaw   _____

5. **concealed** the path to the lake
   a. indicated   b. qualified   c. thawed   d. burdened   _____

6. a show of **modesty**
   a. vanity   b. response   c. burden   d. consent   _____

Completing the Sentence

From the list of words on pages 24–25, choose the one that best completes each item below. Write the word in the space provided. (You may have to change the word's ending.)

UNEXPECTED DANGER

■ When the hikers set out for the mountain, the weather was just as fine as it had been the _____ day. Little did they know the danger that lay in store for them.

■ They did not realize how _____ their clothes and boots were until an unexpected blizzard hit. The temperature dropped sharply, and their worn-out clothes did not keep them warm.

■ Shivering and lost, they knew how _____ it was to find shelter from the storm.

■ At last they came to a cabin. They knocked on the door but got no _____.

■ Then they tried the door, and it opened. Once they were inside, the hikers began to _____ themselves by the wood stove.

■ They used towels they found stored in a _____ to dry themselves off. Before the hikers left the cabin, they wrote a note thanking the cabin's owner.

ADOPTING A PET

■ For months we asked our parents to agree to let us get a dog. We were very excited when they finally _____ to let us have one.

■ "We'll be very _____ pet owners," we promised. "We'll feed the dog and walk it and play with it every day."

■ "If I notice anything to _____ that you are not taking good care of the dog, we will have to give it away," our dad warned.

■ At the pound the vet asked us lots of questions to find out whether we were fit to adopt a dog. We found that not all people _____.

■ "Some pets can be a _____," she explained. "Good intentions are not enough. But you seem ready to accept the responsibility."

■ We looked at a lot of dogs before we found the one that was right for us. We think we picked the most _____ dog there, one with beautiful golden fur and sparkling brown eyes.

 *Circle the letter next to the word or expression that best completes the sentence or answers the question. Pay special attention to the word in **boldface**.*

1. To **indicate** a place on a map, you might
   a. take a picture of it
   b. look it up in an atlas
   c. point it out
   d. write down its name

2. Which is *not* **attractive** to cats?
   a. some fish
   b. some birds
   c. some catnip
   d. some dogs

3. Don't expect **consent** for a class
   a. poetry reading
   b. meeting
   c. fireworks display
   d. project

4. A **dependable** TV would
   a. work all the time
   b. have wavy or rolling lines
   c. break down
   d. blow a fuse

5. If it is May, the **previous** month
   a. was June
   b. was March
   c. was April
   d. was July

6. To **qualify** for a gold medal, you must
   a. have neat handwriting
   b. win the race
   c. speak Latin
   d. have no brothers or sisters

7. A sensible **response** to the question "How are you?" is
   a. "Ten o'clock."
   b. "Some pizza, please."
   c. "Just fine, thanks."
   d. "No thank you."

8. **Shabby** behavior might include
   a. making a new friend
   b. sharing your toys
   c. making rude comments
   d. giving away old clothes

9. Which is an **urgent** situation?
   a. no more popcorn
   b. a grease fire in the kitchen
   c. a chipped fingernail
   d. a sad song on the radio

10. During a March **thaw**, you might
    a. hope spring will arrive early
    b. shovel snow
    c. go swimming in a lake
    d. go ice-skating on a pond

11. You may accuse me of **vanity** if I
    a. help you do your homework
    b. let you borrow my math book
    c. draw a good picture of a horse
    d. boast about my many talents

12. Which is a **burden** to carry?
    a. a ruler
    b. a heavy suitcase
    c. a lunch box
    d. a pair of shoes

Definitions

Study the spelling, pronunciation, part of speech, and definition given for each of the words below. Write the word in the blank space in the sentence that follows. Then read the synonyms and antonyms.

1. **ambush**
   ('am bush)

   (v.) to make a surprise attack from a hidden place
   A small force may try to _____ a larger one.
   (n.) a surprise attack
   A famous _____ took place by that creek.
   SYNONYMS: to attack, trap, waylay; a trap

2. **calculate**
   ('kal kyə lāt)

   (v.) to find out by adding, subtracting, multiplying, or dividing; to figure out by reason or logic
   Let's _____ the full cost of the class trip.
   SYNONYMS: to compute, figure, reckon, evaluate
   ANTONYM: to estimate

3. **contribute**
   (kən 'tri byət)

   (v.) to give money, effort, or items for a cause; to hand in for publication
   Can you _____ some brownies to our bake sale?
   SYNONYMS: to donate, offer, provide; to submit
   ANTONYM: to withhold

4. **dread**
   (dred)

   (v.) to be afraid; to fear or feel deep worry
   Many students _____ surprise tests.
   (n.) deep fear or uneasiness over what may happen
   A _____ of talking in front of others keeps some students from raising their hands in class.
   SYNONYMS: to fear; horror, terror
   ANTONYMS: to welcome, embrace; courage, excitement

5. **employ**
   (im 'ploi)

   (v.) to make use of; to put to work on a job or task for pay
   You may need to _____ a compass in order to draw a perfect circle.
   SYNONYMS: to use, hire, engage
   ANTONYM: to dismiss

6. **extend**
   (ik 'stend)

   (v.) to stretch out, make or last longer; to give or offer
   Let's _____ our vacation into September.
   SYNONYMS: to lengthen, increase, continue, enlarge; to grant
   ANTONYMS: to decrease, lessen, limit; to deny

Figure skaters must practice many hours every day in order to perfect the **routines** (word 9) they will perform in competition.

7. **frantic**
('fran tik)

(adj.) very excited or upset; marked by fast, wild, or nervous action
The scene ended with a _____ search for the lost keys.

SYNONYMS: desperate, frenzied, distracted
ANTONYMS: calm, careful, orderly

8. **initial**
(i 'ni shəl)

(adj.) beginning or first
Our _____ reaction was anger.

(n.) the first letter of a name or word
I picked the _____ H for Hannah.

(v.) to mark or sign with one's initials
Please _____ all papers you correct.

SYNONYMS: first, earliest, opening
ANTONYMS: final, last

9. **routine**
(rü 'tēn)

(n.) the regular or fixed way in which a thing is done; an act or skit
The skaters practiced their _____.

(adj.) normal, predictable, or commonly done; repeated by habit
My _____ morning jog is three miles.

SYNONYMS: a pattern, procedure; ordinary, expected, typical, customary, usual
ANTONYMS: random, irregular, unusual

10. **stun**
(stən)

(v.) to have a sudden, upsetting effect on the mind or feelings; to shock or daze; to make unable to feel, react, or think
Bright lights may _____ a deer for a moment.

SYNONYMS: to astonish, bewilder, deaden, overwhelm, paralyze

11. **sturdy**
('stər dē)

(adj.) firmly or solidly built; determined
A police officer needs a pair of _____ shoes.

SYNONYMS: rugged, hardy, tough, powerful, durable
ANTONYMS: delicate, feeble, weak

12. **yield**
(yēld)

(v.) to give in or give way; to produce or bring forth
I was forced to _____ to her logic.

(n.) the product or amount made or produced
They got a good _____ from the pear trees.

SYNONYMS: to surrender, obey; a harvest, crop
ANTONYM: to resist

Match the Meaning

For each item below choose the word whose meaning is suggested by the clue given. Then write the word in the space provided.

1. To worry deeply over what may happen is to feel a sense of _____.
   a. yield   b. initial   c. dread   d. routine

2. Add columns of numbers to _____ the sum.
   a. extend   b. calculate   c. employ   d. stun

3. Can you _____ any books to our library?
   a. calculate   b. employ   c. contribute   d. stun

4. A surprise attack is a(n) _____.
   a. ambush   b. dread   c. yield   d. routine

5. To be shocked is to be _____.
   a. calculated   b. stunned   c. employed   d. extended

6. I must _____ my arm to reach the top shelf.
   a. dread   b. initial   c. ambush   d. extend

7. To give in to demands is to _____ to them.
   a. ambush   b. extend   c. stun   d. yield

8. The _____ score is the one that comes first.
   a. sturdy   b. routine   c. frantic   d. initial

9. The usual way you do things is your _____.
   a. routine   b. ambush   c. initial   d. yield

10. If I pay you to work for me, I _____ you.
    a. employ   b. calculate   c. ambush   d. extend

11. It takes a(n) _____ bike to handle rough mountain roads.
    a. sturdy   b. frantic   c. initial   d. routine

12. Someone who is very upset may be said to be _____.
    a. frantic   b. initial   c. routine   d. sturdy

Synonyms

*For each item below choose the word that is most nearly the **same** in meaning as the word or phrase in **boldface**. Then write your choice on the line provided.*

1. **bewildered** by an angry reaction
   a. calculated   b. dreaded   c. stunned   d. extended   _____

2. **figure** the damage caused by the flood
   a. contribute   b. calculate   c. employ   d. stun   _____

3. lured into a **trap**
   a. dread   b. initial   c. ambush   d. routine   _____

4. lines that **continue** around the block
   a. ambush   b. dread   c. employ   d. extend   _____

5. an **ordinary** inspection
   a. routine   b. initial   c. sturdy   d. frantic   _____

6. **submit** your best photograph to the newspaper
   a. calculate   b. employ   c. dread   d. contribute   _____

Antonyms

*For each item below choose the word that is most nearly **opposite** in meaning to the word or phrase in **boldface**. Then write your choice on the line provided.*

1. a **calm** reply
   a. routine   b. initial   c. frantic   d. sturdy   _____

2. **dismiss** two new workers
   a. employ   b. ambush   c. stun   d. calculate   _____

3. the **final** letter of her name
   a. initial   b. sturdy   c. frantic   d. routine   _____

4. **welcome** a visit
   a. calculate   b. contribute   c. dread   d. employ   _____

5. a **flimsy** fence
   a. frantic   b. initial   c. routine   d. sturdy   _____

6. ordered them to **resist**
   a. contribute   b. dread   c. yield   d. employ   _____

Completing the Sentence

From the list of words on pages 30–31, choose the one that best completes each item below. Then write the word in the space provided. (You may have to change the word's ending.)

FACING THE UNKNOWN

■ The pioneers who first traveled west carried all of their worldly goods in big, _____ wagons.

■ The normal evening _____ involved building a fire, cooking a meal, feeding the animals, making repairs to their wagons, and trying to get some rest.

■ Some pioneers feared deadly _____ by Native Americans who wanted to protect their lands.

■ Pioneers _____ bad weather, broken gear, and dangerous river crossings.

■ Weary travelers were _____ by how small and rough some frontier settlements really were. For some, the shock was so great that they decided to turn around and return to the East.

■ Parents grew _____ if children got sick, because medicine was scarce.

TIME FOR TIMES

■ "We begin a new unit today with our _____ lesson on multiplying," said the math teacher.

■ Students learned that 4 + 4 + 4 _____ the same answer as 3 × 4.

■ We can _____ the basic facts of multiplication until we learn them by heart.

HOLIDAY KINDNESS

■ The holiday food drive _____ more than ten people. In addition to the people who are paid to organize and lead the drive, many others volunteer to help without any pay at all.

■ Workers take the canned goods that people _____ and deliver them to needy families.

■ This year's food drive will be _____ for an extra week so more people can donate goods.

Word Associations

*Circle the letter next to the word or expression that best completes the sentence or answers the question. Pay special attention to the word in **boldface**.*

1. Soldiers might wait in **ambush** behind a
   a. shopping cart
   b. stop sign
   c. clump of trees
   d. swing set

2. Which would you **calculate**?
   a. sales tax
   b. lunch
   c. a vacation
   d. a bus

3. Which might **stun** you?
   a. a lullaby
   b. a blow to the head
   c. a funny cartoon
   d. a sneeze

4. Most people **dread** hearing
   a. children giggle
   b. birds sing
   c. the television
   d. terrible news

5. To **extend** a supply of paper,
   a. use both sides
   b. buy more pencils
   c. use one side only
   d. sharpen your scissors

6. All restaurants **employ**
   a. outfielders
   b. cooks
   c. judges
   d. dentists

7. The **initial** syllable in the word *supermarket* is
   a. *su*
   b. *per*
   c. *mar*
   d. *ket*

8. You might say I'm **frantic** if I'm
   a. relaxing on the couch
   b. watching television
   c. rushing around the room
   d. doing a crossword puzzle

9. To **contribute** to a good cause,
   a. give three hours of your time
   b. ask to get paid
   c. lock your door
   d. get a haircut

10. Soccer warm-up **routines** include
    a. mowing the grass
    b. shopping for new uniforms
    c. having a play-off game
    d. stretching arms and legs

11. Dairy cows will **yield**
    a. hay
    b. hens
    c. milk
    d. barns

12. Which shoes are most **sturdy**?
    a. flip-flop sandals
    b. hiking boots
    c. high-heeled pumps
    d. fuzzy slippers

 **Selecting Word Meanings**

*For each of the following items circle the choice that is most nearly the **same** in meaning as the word in **boldface**.*

1. carried a great **burden**
   a. book   b. sign   c. treasure   d. load

2. signed a new **contract**
   a. agreement   b. check   c. autograph   d. letter

3. **stunned** by the bad news
   a. amused   b. intrigued   c. dazed   d. annoyed

4. faced many **hardships**
   a. stampedes   b. misfortunes   c. challenges   d. surprises

5. decided to **extend** our trip
   a. cancel   b. delay   c. plan   d. lengthen

6. **calculate** the sale price
   a. ignore   b. figure   c. cancel   d. pay

7. gave their **consent**
   a. permission   b. answer   c. greetings   d. objections

8. a feeling of **dread**
   a. delight   b. weakness   c. fear   d. responsibility

9. serve as our **counsel**
   a. guest   b. lawyer   c. leader   d. representative

10. packed the books in a **sturdy** box
    a. flimsy   b. empty   c. large   d. durable

11. **pledge** to tell the truth
    a. promise   b. forget   c. refuse   d. remember

12. received an **attractive** offer
    a. sincere   b. unusual   c. inviting   d. special

Spelling

For each item below study the **boldface** word in which there is a blank. If a letter is missing, fill in the blank to make a correctly spelled word. If the word is already spelled correctly, leave the blank empty.

1. a friendly **comp__tition**

2. **y__eld** to the majority

3. **spon__or** the event

4. **n__glect** the plants

5. **obtai__n** permission

6. **rout__ne** chores

7. learn **basi__** skills

8. **demonst__ate** the move

9. **e__ploy** an assistant

10. **su__table** behavior

11. **di__miss** the students

12. survived the **amb__ush**

Antonyms

For each of the following items circle the choice that is most nearly the **opposite** in meaning to the word in **boldface**.

1. their **initial** offer
   a. best   b. second   c. final   d. first

2. received a **portion**
   a. whole   b. serving   c. response   d. pledge

3. a **drowsy** audience
   a. noisy   b. tired   c. silent   d. alert

4. **sincere** thanks
   a. heartfelt   b. phony   c. unexpected   d. warm

5. that **vacant** house
   a. occupied   b. beautiful   c. expensive   d. run-down

6. read the **previous** chapter
   a. first   b. following   c. last   d. longest

7. a **stern** voice
   a. deep   b. loud   c. gentle   d. harsh

8. **frantic** crowds of shoppers
   a. tired   b. happy   c. angry   d. orderly

Vocabulary in Context

Words have been left out of the following passage. For each numbered item in the passage, fill in the circle next to the word in the margin that best fills the blank space. Then answer each question below by writing a sentence that contains one of the words you have chosen.

On April 11, 1970, a crew of three confident astronauts went into space on the Apollo 13 mission. There was nothing about the launch to __1__ that anything unexpected might happen. The astronauts were planning another historic walk on the Moon. They had trained for months to prepare for anything they might face during the mission. But no one predicted the __2__ situation they had to deal with when an oxygen tank exploded. This accident nearly crippled the spacecraft.

Of course the astronauts were worried. Their only hope was to stay calm and follow every command the ground crew gave. As highly skilled professionals, the astronauts kept focused on what they had to do. They used all their courage to hide any __3__ feelings when they spoke to Mission Control.

Mission Control experts worked round the clock to plan a rescue. They formed teams to find ways to fix the damaged spacecraft, protect the astronauts, and return them to Earth. Their quick __4__ kept the emergency from turning into a terrible disaster. On April 17, the astronauts splashed down in the Pacific Ocean. Their mission had not gone as planned, but the astronauts had come safely home.

1. ○ qualify
   ○ indicate
   ○ recall
   ○ calculate

2. ○ humble
   ○ vacant
   ○ drowsy
   ○ urgent

3. ○ suitable
   ○ stern
   ○ frantic
   ○ initial

4. ○ response
   ○ competition
   ○ yield
   ○ neglect

5. What was the most important thing about the ground crew's actions?

_____

6. How did conditions on Apollo 13 change after the explosion?

_____

7. What kind of feelings did the courageous astronauts try to hide from the ground crew?

_____

8. Why was the crew of the Apollo 13 confident as they went into space?

_____

Analogies In each of the following circle the letter for the item that best completes the comparison. Then explain the relationship on the lines provided. The first one has been done for you.

1. **annual** is to **yearly** as
   a. previous is to later
   b. weekly is to daily
   c. unpleasant is to attractive
   ⓓ ordinary is to routine

Relationship: <u>"Annual" and "yearly" are</u>

<u>synonyms/have the same meaning;</u>

<u>"ordinary" and "routine" also have the</u>

<u>same meaning.</u>

2. **worn** is to **shabby** as
   a. sturdy is to flimsy
   b. vacant is to empty
   c. fresh is to stale
   d. stern is to gentle

Relationship: _____

_____

_____

3. **essential** is to **unnecessary** as
   a. sincere is to false
   b drowsy is to tired
   c. vanity is to conceit
   d. promise is to pledge

Relationship: _____

_____

_____

_____

4. **heat** is to **thaw** as
   a. rain is to dry
   b. ice is to warm
   c. cold is to freeze
   d. snow is to burn

Relationship: _____

_____

_____

Challenge: Make up your own

Write a comparison using the words in the box below. (Hint: There are three possible analogies.) Then write the relationship on the lines provided. One comparison has been completed for you.

ladder	essential	fish	robin
tuna	stair	hardship	basic
burden	rung	bird	step

Analogy: _____robin_____ is to _____bird_____ as _____tuna_____ is to _____fish_____.

Relationship: <u>A robin is a type of bird. A tuna is a type of fish.</u>

Analogy: _____ is to _____ as _____ is to _____.

Relationship: _____

Word Families

*The words in **boldface** in the sentences below are related to words introduced in Units 1–4. For example, the nouns* calculations *and* contributions *in item 1 are related to the verbs* calculate *and* contribute *(both in Unit 4). Based on your understanding of the unit words, circle the related word in **boldface** that best completes each sentence.*

demonstrate	attractive	sincere	indicate	vacant
neglect	qualify	consent	response	burden
urgent	contribute	competition	dreadful	extend
counsel	suitable	dependable	employ	calculate

1. The generous (**calculations/contributions**) helped us to buy a VCR for our class.

2. It is the job of a (**competitor/counselor**) to give useful advice.

3. The point of the (**demonstration/vacancy**) was to show support for the workers.

4. Baby-sitters known for their (**dependability/employment**) are very popular with the families in our town.

5. In many labs, scientists are testing the (**urgency/suitability**) of new medicines for treating the common cold.

6. Are you sure you are ready to accept the (**burdensome/neglectful**) duties of caring for a pet?

7. Brown leaves can be an (**attraction/indication**) that a plant is getting too much water.

8. Good writing skills are a key (**qualification/extension**) for many kinds of jobs.

9. The front page of the newspaper showed a photo of a (**dreadful/insincere**) accident.

10. The (**consenting/unresponsive**) audience sat in stony silence after each of the comic's bad jokes.

Use the clue and the given letters to complete each word. Write the missing letters of the word in the appropriate boxes. Then use the circled letters and the drawing to answer the CHALLENGE question below.

1. A quiz show

☐ ☐ M ☐ Ⓞ T ☐ ☐ Ⓞ ☐ ☐

2. You do this when you remember.

Ⓞ ☐ Ⓞ ☐ L ☐

3. To be fit for something

☐ U ☐ Ⓞ ☐ F Ⓞ

4. A weight or hardship

☐ ☐ R ☐ Ⓞ N

5. Ragged or faded

☐ H ☐ Ⓞ B ☐

6. The opposite of expand

C ☐ ☐ ☐ ☐ A ☐ Ⓞ

Challenge:

If this sign is on my dressing room door, what am I?

☐ ☐ ☐ ☐ ☐ ☐ ☐ ☐ ☐

UNIT 5

Definitions

Study the spelling, pronunciation, part of speech, and definition given for each of the words below. Write the word in the blank space in the sentence that follows. Then read the synonyms and antonyms.

1. **antique**
(an 'tēk)

(n.) an object made long ago; something made in the past
Some people fill their homes with _____.
(adj.) from the past; very old
The _____ cradle was carved in 1847.

SYNONYMS: an heirloom, relic; ancient, old-fashioned, vintage
ANTONYMS: modern, new, current, fresh

2. **baggage**
('ba gij)

(n.) suitcases, bags, packages, equipment, or other items travelers carry; things that get in the way
Many travelers carry too much _____.

SYNONYMS: luggage, trunks; a hindrance, burden, impediment

3. **digest**
(n., 'dī jest;
v., dī 'jest)

(n.) a shortened version of previously published writings; a magazine that publishes such short versions
My parents read a monthly _____ of international news.
(v.) to understand or grasp an idea; to break down food within the body for nourishment; to make a short summary
You may need time to _____ the lessons you learned in school this week.

SYNONYMS: a summary; to absorb, assimilate, eat, consume, condense, summarize
ANTONYMS: an extension, expansion; to enlarge, expand; to misunderstand

4. **establish**
(is 'ta blish)

(v.) to set up, start, organize, or bring about; to prove beyond doubt
The new baby's parents will _____ a fund for her college education.

SYNONYMS: to build, create, form, plant; to confirm, demonstrate, show
ANTONYMS: to destroy, ruin; to disprove

5. **eternal**
(i 'tər nəl)

(adj.) lasting for all time; with no beginning or end; continuing forever; seeming to be endless
Poets write of the _____ promise of spring.

SYNONYMS: everlasting; timeless; constant, permanent; continual
ANTONYMS: temporary, ending; brief, fleeting, short; changeable

6. **haste**
(hāst)

(n.) speed or quickness of motion; overeager action without caution
If you work in _____, you may make careless mistakes.

SYNONYMS: hurry, swiftness; rashness, carelessness, recklessness
ANTONYMS: slowness, delay; caution

Aviation **pioneers** (word 10) Orville and Wilbur Wright were the first to achieve controlled, powered flight and to build a practical airplane.

7. **humid**
   ('hyü məd)

   (adj.) steamy or heavy with moisture; moist or damp
   Icy lemonade is a refreshing treat on a _____ day.
   SYNONYMS: muggy, soggy, sweltering; wet, clammy
   ANTONYMS: dry, arid

8. **lash**
   (lash)

   (v.) to whip or strike; to scold; to strap down with rope or cord
   A cornered animal may _____ out in fear.
   (n.) a whip; a blow made by or as if by a whip; an eyelash
   The man bore scars from the cruel _____.
   SYNONYMS: to flog, wave, thrash, hit; to tie, secure, fasten; to criticize, abuse
   ANTONYMS: to caress, pat; to untie; to compliment, praise

9. **oppose**
   (ə 'pōz)

   (v.) to act or speak out against, resist, object to; to be in direct contrast with
   A group of senators will _____ the bill.
   SYNONYMS: to protest, fight, dispute, confront; to deny, combat, contradict
   ANTONYMS: to aid, assist, approve, confirm, cooperate, favor, help, support, join

10. **pioneer**
    (pī ə 'nir)

    (n.) a person or group that goes first to explore, open, prepare, or settle an area; someone who breaks new ground, as in science or ideas
    Jacques Cousteau was a _____ in exploring the ocean's depths.
    (v.) to open the way for others to follow; to lead, be the first
    Our city will _____ the use of electric buses.

11. **sensible**
    ('sen sə bəl)

    (adj.) showing or having good judgment or reason; aware of
    It's only _____ to wear a warm coat on a cold day.
    SYNONYMS: reasonable, wise, prudent; informed, conscious, observant
    ANTONYMS: foolish, unwise, unreasonable; unaware

12. **worthy**
    ('wər thē)

    (adj.) having value, importance, or worth; good enough for
    Many people volunteer to work for a _____ charity.
    SYNONYMS: deserving, excellent, good, admirable, useful
    ANTONYMS: worthless, unworthy, useless

Match the Meaning

For each item below choose the word whose meaning is suggested by the clue given. Then write the word in the space provided.

1. A person who starts a new business _____ it.
   a. lashes   b. opposes   c. digests   d. establishes

2. If you chew your food well, it will be easier to _____.
   a. lash   b. digest   c. establish   d. pioneer

3. When you speak out against something, you _____ it.
   a. digest   b. pioneer   c. oppose   d. establish

4. A table that is two hundred years old may be said to be a(n) _____.
   a. antique   b. baggage   c. digest   d. pioneer

5. Something that lasts forever is _____.
   a. sensible   b. humid   c. worthy   d. eternal

6. The first person to walk on the Moon could be called a space _____.
   a. digest   b. pioneer   c. baggage   d. antique

7. A(n) _____ person shows good judgment and awareness.
   a. sensible   b. eternal   c. pioneer   d. humid

8. The suitcases that I take with me when I go on a trip are my _____.
   a. antiques   b. haste   c. baggage   d. lashes

9. If a magazine buys your poem, the editors must think it is _____ of publication.
   a. humid   b. worthy   c. sensible   d. eternal

10. _____ weather is steamy and damp.
    a. Antique   b. Eternal   c. Sensible   d. Humid

11. In an emergency it may be important to act in _____.
    a. pioneer   b. lash   c. haste   d. antique

12. When someone scolds you, they may be said to _____ you with words.
    a. lash   b. establish   c. digest   d. pioneer

Synonyms

*For each item below choose the word that is most nearly the **same** in meaning as the word or phrase in **boldface**. Then write your choice on the line provided.*

1. lit a **permanent** flame at the monument
   a. worthy   b. sensible   c. humid   d. eternal   _____

2. weighed down by heavy **packages**
   a. antiques   b. digests   c. pioneers   d. baggage   _____

3. **whipped** the prisoner
   a. lashed   b. pioneered   c. opposed   d. established   _____

4. **absorbed** the meaning of the speech
   a. opposed   b. digested   c. established   d. pioneered   _____

5. clues that may **confirm** who did it
   a. digest   b. lash   c. establish   d. oppose   _____

6. worked for **deserving** causes
   a. worthy   b. humid   c. antique   d. eternal   _____

Antonyms

*For each item below choose the word that is most nearly **opposite** in meaning to the word or phrase in **boldface**. Then write your choice on the line provided.*

1. a very **unwise** decision
   a. eternal   b. worthy   c. humid   d. sensible   _____

2. **supported** the candidate
   a. pioneered   b. opposed   c. lashed   d. established   _____

3. a set of **new** dishes
   a. antique   b. worthy   c. pioneer   d. sensible   _____

4. a **dry** climate
   a. eternal   b. worthy   c. humid   d. sensible   _____

5. an eager **follower**
   a. pioneer   b. antique   c. digest   d. lash   _____

6. moved with **caution**
   a. baggage   b. pioneers   c. lashes   d. haste   _____

Completing the Sentence

From the list of words on pages 42–43, choose the one that best completes each item below. Write the word in the space provided. (You may have to change the word's ending.)

TIPS FOR HIKERS

■ My friends and I love to hike, even on hot, sticky days. An experienced hiker gave us tips for staying comfortable in such _____ weather.

■ To begin with, _____ a plan and stick to it. Don't waste your energy.

■ Wear hats and sunscreen, drink lots of fluids, and never move in _____. Take your time; and always stop to rest when you feel tired.

A BIG STEP

■ I think of my great grandfather as a _____ because he was the first person from his tiny village to come to America.

■ At first his parents _____ his decision. They worried about what would happen to him in a country where he knew no one and could not speak the language.

■ Finally he convinced them that seeking a better life was a _____ and admirable goal in spite of the risks and uncertainties.

■ Grandfather filled his _____ with clothes and tools. All of the belongings he would take with him he fit into two large trunks.

■ He _____ his favorite books together with a leather strap and hung it over his shoulder.

■ Then he tucked his _____ watch safely in his pocket, said his good-byes, and started on his journey.

GOOD ADVICE

■ Like all living creatures, people have an _____ need for nourishment.

■ When we _____ our food, our bodies turn it into the energy that keeps us going.

■ Doctors offer this very _____ advice: Eat a variety of healthy foods, avoid too much sugar and fat, and drink lots of water.

Word Associations

*Circle the letter next to the word or expression that best completes the sentence or answers the question. Pay special attention to the word in **boldface**.*

1. To be **worthy** of the lead in the play, you should
   a. know how to sew costumes
   b. have a clear speaking voice
   c. be good in science and math
   d. have perfect attendance

2. Something **eternal** would
   a. last a while
   b. stop suddenly
   c. last forever
   d. stop before it starts

3. A **sensible** pet for an apartment
   a is a Shetland pony
   b. is a seal
   c. is a St. Bernard dog
   d. is a hamster

4. The **baggage** for my trip holds
   a. my hotel room
   b. my airplane seat
   c. my bathtub
   d. my pajamas

5. Most **pioneers** would wonder
   a. how to survive in a new area
   b. when to phone home
   c. where to get good pizza
   d. what time it is

6. Which of these is an **antique**?
   a. a cellular phone
   b. a Civil War sword
   c. a CD player
   d. a new car

7. To **establish** a good relationship, neighbors might
   a. play loud music late at night
   b. ruin each other's gardens
   c. break each other's windows
   d. smile and say hello

8. If someone **lashes** out at you,
   a. they scold you severely
   b. they ask you for directions
   c. they give you a gift
   d. they drive you to the mall

9. A science **digest** might print a
   a. recipe for lasagna
   b. long science-fiction novel
   c. summary of a medical study
   d. complete play about Dr. Seuss

10. To **oppose** closing the old library,
    a. speak out in public to save it
    b. return your overdue books
    c. get a wrecking ball
    d. move to another town

11. In a **humid** place, you might
    a. have a garage
    b. have damp towels
    c. have a credit card
    d. have a picnic

12. Which animal often moves in **haste**?
    a. a snail
    b. a turtle
    c. a rabbit
    d. a sloth

Definitions

Study the spelling, pronunciation, part of speech, and definition given for each of the words below. Write the word in the blank space in the sentence that follows. Then read the synonyms and antonyms.

1. **blossom**
   ('blä səm)

   (n.) a flower or group of flowers; the state or time of flowering
   A rose garden in _____ sweetens the air.
   (v.) to have or produce flowers; to develop, open up, or appear
   Steady encouragement can help a person's talent to _____.
   SYNONYMS: a bloom, bud; to unfold, flourish, grow
   ANTONYMS: to shrink, wither, fade

2. **collide**
   (kə 'līd)

   (v.) to bump into hard, come together with force; to clash
   Small meteors sometimes _____ with the Moon.
   SYNONYMS: to crash, smash, hit, slam; to conflict
   ANTONYMS: to avoid, evade, elude; to agree, consent, settle

3. **constant**
   ('kän stənt)

   (adj.) never stopping; happening over and over again; staying the same; loyal, steady, or faithful
   City dwellers get used to the _____ hum of traffic.
   (n.) something that does not change or vary
   The need for food is a _____ for all living things.
   SYNONYMS: continuous, unchanging, endless, regular, uninterrupted; true, trusty
   ANTONYMS: variable, changeable, irregular, random; faithless, fickle

4. **content**
   (*adj.,* kən 'tent;
   n., 'kän tent)

   (adj.) pleased with or accepting of; not wanting anything else
   Our neighbors are _____ with their new home.
   (n.) an amount that is held or contained; the meaning or subject of
   The _____ of that book is too technical for me.
   SYNONYMS: satisfied, comfortable, fulfilled; the gist, theme
   ANTONYMS: dissatisfied, unhappy, restless; discontent

5. **distract**
   (di 'strakt)

   (v.) to draw attention to something else or cause to turn aside; to confuse or disturb
   Try not to let the noise _____ you.
   SYNONYMS: to divert, sidetrack, interfere; to disturb, bother, interrupt
   ANTONYMS: to focus, explain, concentrate

6. **drought**
   (draut)

   (n.) a long time without rain; a prolonged shortage
   Farmers lost their entire crops because of the _____.
   SYNONYMS: dryness; lack
   ANTONYMS: a drenching, flood; a surplus, glut

7. **foul**
('faúl')

(adj.) unpleasant to the senses; dirty, clogged, or polluted; dishonorable; against the rules of a sport or game; stormy or rainy
The criminal was responsible for many _____ deeds.

(n.) a violation of the rules; a ball that goes outside boundary lines
The umpire ruled that the ball was a _____.

(v.) to pollute or make filthy; to break the rules of a game; to hit a foul
Leaky oil tanks can _____ water and soil.

SYNONYMS: offensive, nasty, smelly; a violation; to soil, contaminate
ANTONYMS: attractive, clean, clear, fair, honest, pleasant, pure; to clean, purify

8. **noble**
('no bəl')

(adj.) of high birth or rank; outstanding, of good moral character
The hero of the play is a _____ lord.

(n.) someone of high rank or birth
A commoner may gain a title by marrying a _____.

SYNONYMS: highborn; honorable; lofty, splendid, majestic; an aristocrat
ANTONYMS: base, ignoble, lowly; a commoner

9. **policy**
('pä lə sē')

(n.) a plan, set of rules, or way to act; a written insurance contract
The store changed its refund _____.

SYNONYMS: guidelines, procedures; a code, system, practice

10. **quiver**
('kwi vər')

(n.) a case used to hold arrows; a trembling or shaking motion
Only one arrow was left in the archer's _____.

(v.) to shake or tremble
When I am nervous, my hands _____.

SYNONYMS: a sheath; a tremor, shiver; to tremble, shudder, flutter, quake, vibrate

11. **slight**
(slīt)

(adj.) small in size or degree; not much; not important
There may be _____ delays in train service.

(v.) to treat as unimportant; to make light of
A good host and hostess never _____ their guests.

(n.) an act of neglect or discourtesy
I apologized for the unintentional _____.

SYNONYMS: slender, minor, trivial; to neglect, snub; an insult
ANTONYMS: husky, muscular, large, strong; important, major; a compliment

12. **tidy**
('tī dē')

(adj.) neat and in good order; comfortable or large in amount
I was surprised to receive a _____ reward.

(v.) to put things in neat or proper order
Be sure to _____ the room before you go.

SYNONYMS: orderly, clean, trim; generous, large, substantial; to neaten, organize
ANTONYMS: messy, disordered, dirty, sloppy; small; to litter, jumble, clutter, confuse

Match the Meaning

For each item below choose the word whose meaning is suggested by the clue given. Then write the word in the space provided.

1. Something that takes your attention away from your homework may be said to
   _____ you.
   a. collide   b. quiver   c. slight   d. distract

2. When the cherry trees _____ it is a sure sign of spring.
   a. distract   b. blossom   c. quiver   d. collide

3. To shake is to _____.
   a. slight   b. distract   c. quiver   d. distract

4. A guide dog is the blind person's _____ partner.
   a. constant   b. content   c. foul   d. tidy

5. If your closet is neat and organized, it is _____.
   a. slight   b. noble   c. foul   d. tidy

6. Stormy weather may be described as _____.
   a. constant   b. foul   c. noble   d. slight

7. A _____ is an act of discourtesy.
   a. slight   b. blossom   c. foul   d. noble

8. A long period of time without rain is called a _____.
   a. constant   b. policy   c. drought   d. quiver

9. When skaters _____, they bump into each other with force.
   a. blossom   b. collide   c. distract   d. quiver

10. A person of good moral character may perform _____ acts.
    a. constant   b. tidy   c. slight   d. noble

11. Rules on how to act on the job form the company's _____ for workers.
    a. blossom   b. content   c. policy   d. drought

12. People who are _____ with their lives feel happy and satisfied.
    a. content   b. constant   c. slight   d. noble

Synonyms

*For each item below choose the word that is most nearly the **same** in meaning as the word or phrase in **boldface.** Then write your choice on the line provided.*

1. flowers that **flutter** in the breeze
   a. quiver   b. blossom   c. distract   d. collide   _____

2. a **highborn** family
   a. tidy   b. content   c. noble   d. slight   _____

3. **contaminate** the water supply
   a. slight   b. quiver   c. distract   d. foul   _____

4. saw the players **crash**
   a. collide   b. blossom   c. distract   d. quiver   _____

5. the **theme** of the story
   a. slight   b. content   c. policy   d. quiver   _____

6. an insurance **contract**
   a. drought   b. constant   c. policy   d. blossom   _____

Antonyms

*For each item below choose the word that is most nearly **opposite** in meaning to the word or phrase in **boldface.** Then write your choice on the line provided.*

1. **withers** on the vine
   a. collides   b. blossoms   c. quivers   d. distracts   _____

2. a **messy** room
   a. foul   b. slight   c. tidy   d. noble   _____

3. an unexpected **compliment**
   a. blossom   b. quiver   c. policy   d. slight   _____

4. **focus** the students' attention
   a. collide   b. slight   c. distract   d. blossom   _____

5. a **flood** of good ideas
   a. slight   b. quiver   c. policy   d. drought   _____

6. a **fickle** friend
   a. tidy   b. constant   c. noble   d. slight   _____

Completing the Sentence

From the list of words on pages 48–49, choose the one that best completes each item below. Write the word in the space provided. (You may have to change the word's ending.)

DRY TIMES

■ Last year there was almost no rain in our state. No one knew how long the _____ would last.

■ For many months the weather was unusually hot. The _____ heat dried up fields and gardens.

■ Withered leaves and plants _____ in the hot breezes. It was a sad sight.

■ Many farmers lost their crops. Apple growers were especially hard hit. Most of their trees did not _____. When it was time for the harvest, there were only a few apples to pick.

AN UNPLEASANT TASK

■ Everyone in my family has a regular household job to do. Mine is keeping the refrigerator clean and _____.

■ I am supposed to check the _____ of the refrigerator once a week. But last week I forgot to do it.

■ My mom was very annoyed. She asked me to make the "_____" effort to clean up the mess.

■ A _____ odor hit my nose when I opened the door. What was that disgusting thing at the back of the shelf? My science project? No, it was just a moldy sandwich that I forgot to take to school.

SAFETY IN THE PARK

■ Everyone enjoys our city park. That means the park can get very crowded, especially on weekends. All that activity can _____ people, and quite a few have been hurt.

■ To cut down on the number of accidents, the mayor has put a park safety _____ into effect.

■ Skaters and bicycle riders are required to slow down when they get near a crosswalk. This rule is intended to keep them from _____ with people who are trying to get to the other side of the road.

■ If people follow the rules and stay alert, their chances of being injured are _____.

*Circle the letter next to the word or expression that best completes the sentence or answers the question. Pay special attention to the word in **boldface**.*

1. When two baseball players **collide**, they
   a. shake hands
   b. tell jokes
   c. crash into each other
   d. sing the national anthem

2. You can **tidy** up the kitchen by
   a. having a dinner party
   b. watering the plants
   c. opening the windows
   d. washing the dirty dishes

3. Which might develop a **blossom**?
   a. a lightbulb
   b. a magnolia tree
   c. a cup of tea
   d. a baseball glove

4. During a **drought** you will see
   a. wilted plants
   b. open umbrellas
   c. green lawns
   d. deep puddles

5. A **quivering** puppy might be
   a. sleepy
   b. cold
   c. running
   d. growing

6. If I walk at a **constant** rate,
   a. I won't cross the street
   b. I won't get lost
   c. I won't go faster or slower
   d. I won't get thirsty

7. If something **distracts** me, it
   a. gives me a toothache
   b. interrupts my thoughts
   c. makes me hungry
   d. helps me to study

8. If I am **content** with my homework, I
   a. lose it
   b. do it over
   c. read it out loud
   d. hand it in

9. A **noble** might live in a
   a. palace
   b. tent
   c. homeless shelter
   d. houseboat

10. When a ball is **foul**, it
    a. breaks a window
    b. goes into the goal
    c. goes out of bounds
    d. doesn't bounce

11. To **slight** your cousins, you might
    a. ignore them
    b. grow taller than they are
    c. hug them
    d. bring them gifts

12. Which of these is a **policy**?
    a. a menu
    b. a timetable
    c. a movie ticket
    d. a dress code

UNIT 7

Definitions

Study the spelling, pronunciation, part of speech, and definition given for each of the words below. Write the word in the blank space in the sentence that follows. Then read the synonyms and antonyms.

1. **accurate**
('a kyə rət)

(adj.) without errors, completely correct; conforming to the truth
It is important to take _____ notes in class.

SYNONYMS: exact, precise; true, careful
ANTONYMS: mistaken, wrong, false, questionable, misleading; inaccurate, careless

2. **alert**
(ə 'lərt)

(adj.) watchful and ready to act; quick to understand and act
A good watchdog is _____ and protective.

(n.) readiness; an alarm; a time when an alarm is in effect
Police and firefighters are always on _____.

(v.) to warn or make aware of
Signs on a highway _____ drivers of hazards.

SYNONYMS: attentive, vigilant; a signal; to notify, inform
ANTONYMS: inattentive, unobservant, unaware

3. **ancestor**
('an ses tər)

(n.) a family member who lived at an earlier time
You may want to study the lives of your _____.

SYNONYMS: a forerunner, forebear, forefather, foremother
ANTONYM: a descendant

4. **disaster**
(di 'zas tər)

(n.) a sudden, terrible event that brings great damage or suffering; a great failure
It took months to recover from the _____.

SYNONYMS: a tragedy, catastrophe, calamity, misfortune, trouble
ANTONYMS: a success, triumph

5. **elementary**
(e lə 'men tə rē)

(adj.) related to the simplest or beginning level of something
Beginning students of the piano practice _____ pieces to develop their skills.

SYNONYMS: basic, beginning, fundamental, introductory
ANTONYMS: complex, hard, difficult, advanced

6. **envy**
('en vē)

(n.) a feeling of resentment caused by longing for what someone has; a person or object that is envied
Our team's winning season was the _____ of the league.

(v.) to resent and want what someone else has
There may be times when you _____ another person's good luck in life.

SYNONYMS: jealousy, desire, greed; to covet, begrudge
ANTONYM: satisfaction

54

7. **epidemic**
   (e pə 'de mik)

(adj.) spreading to a very large group at the same time; contagious
   Polio was once _____ *in the United States.*

(n.) a rapid and widespread outbreak of a disease; sudden rapid growth or development
   An _____ *of Dutch elm disease destroyed hundreds of trees in our town park.*

SYNONYMS: catching, infectious; rife, widespread, universal; an infection, plague
ANTONYMS: isolated, contained, limited

8. **feeble**
   ('fē bəl)

(adj.) having little strength or force; without energy or authority
   The exhausted runner managed to give us a _____ *smile after the long race.*

SYNONYMS: weak, frail, faint, fragile
ANTONYMS: able, strong, forceful, powerful; energetic

9. **penetrate**
   ('pe nə trāl)

(v.) to enter or force a way through or into; to see into
   Cars are equipped with special lights that can _____ *fog.*

SYNONYMS: to pass through, pierce, puncture; to see; to grasp, realize
ANTONYMS: to withdraw; to misunderstand

10. **romp**
    (rämp)

(n.) spirited, carefree, or noisy fun; something that suggests merry play
   The class enjoyed a _____ *in the playground.*

(v.) to run or play in a lively or carefree way; to win easily
   We watched the puppies _____ *on the lawn.*

SYNONYMS: a lark, frolic, sport, caper; to caper, frolic, skip, bound

11. **staple**
    ('stā pəl)

(n.) a U-shaped wire that fastens material by piercing and bending; a major product, material, part, or item regularly used
   Fruits and vegetables are _____ *of a healthy diet.*

(v.) to fasten with staples
   Please _____ *the pages of your report together.*

(adj.) chief, principal; needed or used regularly
   Rice is a _____ *crop in many Asian countries.*

SYNONYMS: necessities; basics; basic, main, important, essential
ANTONYMS: nonessentials; minor, unnecessary

12. **survive**
    (sər 'vīv)

(v.) to stay alive or continue to exist; to keep on going; to live longer than
   We need food and shelter in order to _____ .

SYNONYMS: to live, persist; to endure, last, withstand; to outlive
ANTONYMS: to die, perish

Match the Meaning

For each item below choose the word whose meaning is suggested by the clue given. Then write the word in the space provided.

1. If a team wins a game easily, it may be said to _____ over its opponents.
   a. survive   b. penetrate   c. envy   d. romp

2. If I wish I had the advantages that someone else enjoys, I _____ that person.
   a. alert   b. envy   c. survive   d. staple

3. To pierce or enter something is to _____ it.
   a. alert   b. survive   c. penetrate   d. envy

4. A widespread outbreak of a disease is called an _____.
   a. epidemic   b. alert   c. envy   d. ancestor

5. The _____ lessons are the easiest ones.
   a. accurate   b. feeble   c. staple   d. elementary

6. The major product produced in a state may be called a(n) _____.
   a. alert   b. staple   c. disaster   d. epidemic

7. A(n) _____ watch shows the exact time.
   a. accurate   b. elementary   c. alert   d. feeble

8. Members of your family who lived in the distant past are called your _____.
   a. epidemics   b. disasters   c. ancestors   d. romps

9. If you stay alive or keep going, you _____.
   a. envy   b. survive   c. romp   d. penetrate

10. An action that lacks strength and authority is a(n) _____ effort.
    a. accurate   b. elementary   c. staple   d. feeble

11. A severe storm that causes great property damage is a natural _____.
    a. envy   b. romp   c. disaster   d. ancestor

12. If I am _____, I am watchful and ready for whatever happens.
    a. alert   b. feeble   c. accurate   d. elementary

Synonyms

*For each item below choose the word that is most nearly the **same** in meaning as the word or phrase in **boldface**. Then write your choice on the line provided.*

1. an **introductory** class in astronomy
   a. accurate   b. epidemic   c. feeble   d. elementary   _____

2. a **plague** of unknown cause
   a. alert   b. epidemic   c. ancestor   d. romp   _____

3. **passed through** enemy lines
   a. penetrated   b. envied   c. alerted   d. survived   _____

4. **covets** the prize
   a. penetrates   b. envies   c. survives   d. staples   _____

5. **skipped** along
   a. survived   b. alerted   c. romped   d. penetrated   _____

6. financial **catastrophes**
   a. ancestors   b. romps   c. staples   d. disasters   _____

Antonyms

*For each item below choose the word that is most nearly **opposite** in meaning to the word or phrase in **boldface**. Then write your choice on the line provided.*

1. not expected to **die**
   a. romp   b. survive   c. envy   d. penetrate   _____

2. **misleading** information about the law
   a. alert   b. elementary   c. feeble   d. accurate   _____

3. made a **strong** effort
   a. accurate   b. feeble   c. alert   d. elementary   _____

4. an **inattentive** audience
   a. alert   b. staple   c. accurate   d. feeble   _____

5. bought many **unnecessary** items
   a. feeble   b. alert   c. staple   d. accurate   _____

6. **descendants** of the pioneers
   a. ancestors   b. disasters   c. epidemics   d. staples   _____

Completing the Sentence

From the list of words on pages 54–55, choose the one that best completes each item below. Write the word in the space provided. (You may have to change the word's ending.)

THE QUICKNESS OF SICKNESS

■ News reports predicted that this winter's flu _____ would be very bad.

■ Our state's health department tried to _____ people to the importance of getting their flu shots as early as possible. Unfortunately the disease spread so quickly that many people did not have a chance to protect themselves.

■ The symptoms of this year's strain of flu left even strong people _____ and unable to take care of themselves.

MUSIC AND LEARNING

■ Music can be an important teaching tool in the _____ school classroom.

■ Singing and movement are recognized as _____ of young children's learning, almost as essential as reading and arithmetic.

■ Songs can help children to remember such things as the alphabet. Musical games that involve movement may be a(n) _____ for the youngsters. But they also help children to develop good physical coordination.

■ Learning to play a simple instrument can help children to develop a(n) _____ sense of rhythm and to learn to count.

NO WARNING

■ The story of my mother's _____ is dramatic. They settled in the Pennsylvania city of Johnstown in the early 1800s.

■ They did well in business and lived comfortably. According to family legend, their beautiful house was the _____ of their neighbors for decades. But in an instant, all of that changed.

■ On May 31, 1889, a terrible _____ struck Johnstown. A dam collapsed, sending a deadly flood through the city.

■ When rescue workers were able to _____ the wreckage, they found terrible destruction. More than two thousand people had been killed, and the damage to property was widespread.

■ My mother's family was more fortunate than many. They lost all their material possessions, but they _____. They knew that as long as they were together, they could rebuild their lives.

*Circle the letter next to the word or expression that best completes the sentence or answers the question. Pay special attention to the word in **boldface**.*

1. If my math homework is **accurate**, I have made
   a. many mistakes
   b. several mistakes
   c. two mistakes
   d. no mistakes

2. In **elementary** school you find
   a. kindergarten students
   b. college students
   c. twelfth graders
   d. eighth graders

3. Plants that **survive** the winter
   a. are delicate
   b. are sturdy
   c. are flowery
   d. are dead

4. Tools that **penetrate** wood must
   a. be expensive
   b. be new
   c. be sharp
   d. be curved

5. During an **epidemic**, you might
   a. catch chicken pox
   b. become a doctor
   c. get very hungry
   d. go to the mall

6. Your neighbors may **envy** your
   a. broken windows
   b. rusty old car
   c. beautiful lawn
   d. crabgrass

7. Which of these **alerts** you in case of fire?
   a. a smoke detector
   b. an alarm clock
   c. a personal stereo
   d. an E-mail message

8. Which is a **disaster**?
   a. an earthworm
   b. an earthling
   c. an earthmover
   d. an earthquake

9. A **staple** product of Hawaii is
   a. pinecones
   b. pineapples
   c. pumpkins
   d. pizza

10. A mammoth is whose **ancestor**?
    a. the chipmunk
    b. the cave dwellers
    c. your grandparents
    d. the elephant

11. A **feeble** argument would
    a. not convince anybody
    b. cause a war
    c. last for a few weeks
    d. involve lots of yelling

12. Who is probably having a **romp**?
    a. a man working in a library
    b. a boy sitting and weeping
    c. a girl doing cartwheels
    d. a woman driving a truck

Definitions

Study the spelling, pronunciation, part of speech, and definition given for each of the words below. Write the word in the blank space in the sentence that follows. Then read the synonyms and antonyms.

1. **awkward**
('ô kwərd)

(adj.) not skillful or graceful; hard to handle; embarrassing

When you first learn to dance, your movements may be _____.

SYNONYMS: clumsy, ungainly, bumbling, inept, unskilled; difficult, unmanageable
ANTONYMS: graceful, skillful, pleasant, handy; manageable

2. **clatter**
('kla tər)

(v.) to make short, sharp sounds by rattling or banging together; to speak or move with confused, noisy sound

The old trains _____ as they move down the tracks.

(n.) a hard, rattling sound; busy excitement; noisy chattering

The _____ of machines in some factories is extremely loud.

SYNONYMS: to rattle, chatter; a racket, commotion

3. **gallant**
(*n.,* gə 'lant;
adj., 'ga lənt)

(adj.) showy in appearance; splendid; brave or full of spirit, showing courtesy; very attentive

We saw the parade of _____ sailing ships.

(n.) a fashionable young gentleman; a suitor

The heroine of the novel was courted by a wealthy _____.

SYNONYMS: splendid, dashing; valiant, heroic, daring; polite, considerate, chivalrous
ANTONYMS: afraid, cowardly, timid; selfish, rude; a slob, hobo

4. **lukewarm**
('lük wôrm)

(adj.) only moderately warm, not hot but not cold; without enthusiasm

A dull speech is likely to get _____ applause.

SYNONYMS: tepid, halfhearted
ANTONYMS: steaming hot, boiling; icy, freezing; eager, enthusiastic

5. **plentiful**
('plen ti fəl)

(adj.) in great supply, easily available; more than enough

Flowers are _____ in springtime.

SYNONYMS: ample, abundant, bountiful
ANTONYMS: scarce, rare, meager

6. **ration**
('ra shən)

(n.) a portion of food allowed for one meal or one day; food or supplies; a share

A soup kitchen provides _____ to the poor.

(v.) to pass out in limited portions; to limit the use of

When water is scarce, people must _____ it.

SYNONYMS: an allowance, share, allotment; provisions; to parcel, divide, dispense

7. **reserve**
(ri 'zərv)

(v.) to hold back or set aside; to save for future use
Please _____ a seat for me.

(n.) something set aside for a certain purpose; something stored for later use; the use of care or caution in actions or words
We watched the squirrel dig up its _____ of nuts.

SYNONYMS: to store, retain, stash, withhold; a supply, stock; restraint, composure
ANTONYMS: to splurge, squander, waste, use; boldness, warmth

8. **scholar**
('skä lər)

(n.) a learned person; an expert in a field of study; someone who studies with a teacher; a student who gets a gift of money to pay for education
The book was written by a respected _____.

SYNONYMS: a sage, professor, authority, pupil

9. **smolder**
('smol dər)

(v.) to burn slowly, with smoke but no flame; to exist in a suppressed state; to show suppressed feelings
A person may _____ with rage but say nothing.

SYNONYMS: to simmer, fester, seethe, fume, stew
ANTONYMS: to blaze; to explode

10. **trudge**
('trəj)

(v.) to walk or march slowly and with difficulty or tiredness
At the end of a long day, workers _____ home.

(n.) a long, tiring walk
If I miss the bus, it's a two-mile _____ to school.

SYNONYMS: to plod, slog, tramp; a hike
ANTONYMS: to prance, race, hurry

11. **volunteer**
(vä lən 'tir)

(n.) a person who chooses to join or to do a service; someone who gives time or effort without pay
_____ are needed at the children's hospital.

(v.) to offer one's services; to do or say freely
Who will _____ to set the dinner table?

SYNONYMS: an unpaid person; voluntary; to enlist; to offer
ANTONYMS: an employee, draftee; paid, hired; to force, draft

12. **weary**
('wir ē)

(adj.) feeling tired, worn out; having no more patience
When I have to do a boring task, I become _____.

(v.) to make tired; to grow tired
A dull speech may _____ an audience.

SYNONYMS: exhausted, drained, fatigued, drooping, sleepy
ANTONYMS: fresh, lively, energetic; tolerant; to enliven, energize

Match the Meaning

For each item below choose the word whose meaning is suggested by the clue given. Then write the word in the space provided.

1. A measured portion of food is called a _____.
   a. clatter   b. gallant   c. trudge   d. ration

2. A fire that burns without flame but with smoke _____.
   a. volunteers   b. reserves   c. smolders   d. clatters

3. If you have to _____ through deep snow, your journey will be difficult.
   a. volunteer   b. trudge   c. ration   d. scholar

4. A(n) _____ action is one that is courteous and brave.
   a. gallant   b. awkward   c. lukewarm   d. weary

5. A _____ shower is neither hot nor cold.
   a. plentiful   b. weary   c. gallant   d. lukewarm

6. When horses' hooves clop on the pavement, they can be said to _____.
   a. volunteer   b. clatter   c. reserve   d. trudge

7. A social situation that is embarrassing and hard to handle can be termed _____.
   a. awkward   b. lukewarm   c. plentiful   d. weary

8. An expert in the law may be known as a legal _____.
   a. gallant   b. reserve   c. scholar   d. volunteer

9. If you have more than enough of something, you have a(n) _____ amount.
   a. awkward   b. plentiful   c. weary   d. lukewarm

10. A long period of hard work is likely to leave a person feeling _____.
    a. awkward   b. lukewarm   c. plentiful   d. weary

11. A cook may _____ leftover food to be eaten at a later date.
    a. clatter   b. volunteer   c. reserve   d. smolder

12. If you _____ your services, you will not be paid.
    a. volunteer   b. ration   c. clatter   d. reserve

Synonyms

*For each item below choose the word that is most nearly the **same** in meaning as the word or phrase in **boldface**. Then write your choice on the line provided.*

1. a well-known academic **authority**
   a. gallant   b. volunteer   c. reserve   d. scholar   _____

2. **exhausted** after the race
   a. weary   b. plentiful   c. lukewarm   d. awkward   _____

3. heard the **racket** of the tire chains
   a. reserve   b. scholar   c. ration   d. clatter   _____

4. **plodded** through the mud
   a. smoldered   b. trudged   c. volunteered   d. clattered   _____

5. **gave out** the treats
   a. volunteered   b. clattered   c. rationed   d. smoldered   _____

6. an **unpaid** teacher's aide
   a. gallant   b. volunteer   c. weary   d. lukewarm   _____

Antonyms

*For each item below choose the word that is most nearly **opposite** in meaning to the word or phrase in **boldface**. Then write your choice on the line provided.*

1. **scarce** resources
   a. lukewarm   b. plentiful   c. awkward   d. volunteer   _____

2. a **graceful** gesture
   a. volunteer   b. gallant   c. weary   d. awkward   _____

3. a bowl of **steaming** soup
   a. awkward   b. weary   c. lukewarm   d. plentiful   _____

4. **wasted** our energy
   a. smoldered   b. volunteered   c. reserved   d. clattered   _____

5. watched the logs in the fireplace **blaze**
   a. clatter   b. smolder   c. volunteer   d. trudge   _____

6. **cowardly** behavior
   a. gallant   b. volunteer   c. awkward   d. lukewarm   _____

Completing the Sentence

From the list of words on pages 60–61, choose the one that best completes each item below. Write the word in the space provided. (You may have to change the word's ending.)

A GROUP EFFORT

■ Everyone in town complained that the park was a mess. Our school decided to do something about it. We _____ to clean it up.

■ Last Saturday we got to work. We began by picking up trash. The bottles and cans _____ when we tossed them into recycling bins.

■ Then we went to work on the plants and the lawns. It was _____ for the smaller children to use big brooms and rakes, but they did their best.

■ We gathered all the fallen leaves and sticks and broken branches into a big heap to make a bonfire. One of the teachers lit the pile, and we all watched as it _____ for a while. Finally it burst into flame.

■ By four o'clock, we were _____ and ready to call it a day.

■ We stood back to admire our work. The park looked beautiful! Everyone cheered. Then we _____ home proudly. We were ready for cold drinks and hot showers.

AFTER THE FIGHTING ENDED

■ Many _____ have spent years studying what happened during and after World War II. They have written hundreds of books about what life was like in Europe after the fighting ended.

■ Getting something to eat was difficult. Crops had been destroyed, and many farm animals had been killed or starved to death. _____ were in short supply.

■ Some families had managed to stash a few items in _____, but thousands were hungry.

■ Fuel for heat was very scarce. It was a luxury just to have some _____ water for a bath.

■ Kind and _____ soldiers gave their sweaters and blankets to shivering children and old people.

■ Even though life was hard and people had to struggle to get by, one thing was truly _____: hope for the future.

Word Associations

*Circle the letter next to the word or expression that best completes the sentence or answers the question. Pay special attention to the word in **boldface**.*

1. Someone who feels **awkward** in front of an audience might
   a. try out for the talent show
   b. become an opera singer
   c. join the debating team
   d. avoid the drama club

2. Books are usually **plentiful**
   a. in a zoo
   b. in a library
   c. in a hospital
   d. in a laundromat

3. A **smoldering** home was recently
   a. on fire
   b. painted
   c. sold
   d. built

4. If milk is **rationed**, expect
   a. a small serving of milk
   b. all the juice you want
   c. a glass of water
   d. nothing at all to drink

5. To **reserve** a library book, you
   a. borrow a friend's copy
   b. go to a bookstore
   c. put your name on a list
   d. make a photocopy of it

6. You would measure a **trudge**
   a. by the inch
   b. by the foot
   c. by the yard
   d. by the mile

7. A **gallant** act on a cold day is
   a. to throw snowballs
   b. to zip up your jacket
   c. to offer your gloves to a friend
   d. to stay inside during recess

8. With crowds or traffic **clattering** by, it would be very hard to
   a. cook a healthy supper
   b. find the nearest bus stop
   c. have a quiet conversation
   d. climb a stepladder

9. To **volunteer** information, you'd
   a. join the school band
   b. freely tell what you know
   c. get paid
   d. hire librarians

10. **Weary** tourists might
    a. sit down and rest
    b. get up very early
    c. stay out all night
    d. work out at a gym

11. Which is probably **lukewarm**?
    a. a frosty pitcher of lemonade
    b. an ice-cream cone
    c. a steaming pot of soup
    d. a half-empty mug of cocoa

12. A **scholar** probably spent years
    a. sewing
    b. studying
    c. eating
    d. dancing

Selecting Word Meanings

*For each of the following items circle the choice that is most nearly the **same** in meaning as the word in **boldface.***

1. made the plates **clatter**
   a. slip   b. rattle   c. break   d. drop

2. unable to **penetrate** the surface
   a. clean   b. paint   c. cover   d. pierce

3. the **policy** against smoking
   a. guidelines   b. insurance   c. deadline   d. sign

4. had to **ration** the supplies
   a. store   b. purchase   c. distribute   d. waste

5. a period of severe **drought**
   a. heat   b. rain   c. cold   d. dryness

6. a deadly **epidemic**
   a. infection   b. weapon   c. poison   d. accident

7. **lash** the cartons to the truck
   a. examine   b. carry   c. strap   d. unload

8. **smolder** with anger
   a. speak   b. seethe   c. explode   d. act

9. tucked away in my **baggage**
   a. garbage   b. closet   c. wallet   d. suitcases

10. a **lukewarm** response
    a. half-hearted   b. enthusiastic   c. friendly   d. hostile

11. **content** to stay home
    a. disappointed   b. unable   c. satisfied   d. required

12. tried not to **envy** their success
    a. copy   b. long for   c. notice   d. object to

Spelling

*For each item below study the **boldface** word in which there is a blank. If a letter is missing, fill in the blank to make a correctly spelled word. If the word is already spelled correctly, leave the blank empty.*

1. gave **ac__urate** answers

2. a natural **di__aster**

3. wish for **etern__l** youth

4. **h__mid** air

5. **op__pose** the idea

6. a **plent__ful** harvest

7. **reserv__** the date

8. a respected **sc__olar**

9. **sur__vive** the injury

10. **volun__eer** for the job

11. a **stap__le** of our diet

12. a famous **an__estor**

Antonyms

*For each of the following items circle the choice that is most nearly the **opposite** in meaning to the word in **boldface**.*

1. a **constant** source of energy
   a. continuous   b. instant   c. expensive   d. irregular

2. **gallant** warriors
   a. noble   b. cowardly   c. enemy   d. weary

3. required **haste**
   a. slowness   b. time   c. money   d. speed

4. a **pioneer** in science
   a. trailblazer   b. expert   c. follower   d. student

5. **awkward** on the dance floor
   a. unskilled   b. comic   c. graceful   d. clumsy

6. an **elementary** course
   a. enjoyable   b. advanced   c. interesting   d. difficult

7. **establish** a reputation
   a. question   b. earn   c. build   d. ruin

8. seemed to **blossom** overight
   a. wither   b. disappear   c. flower   d. change

Words have been left out of the following passage. For each numbered item in the passage, fill in the circle next to the word in the margin that best fills the blank space. Then answer each question below by writing a sentence that contains one of the words you have chosen.

People who drive in __1__ weather should be very careful. Snow, sleet, heavy rain, and ice make roads slippery. High winds and fog can make it hard to see. If drivers have to make sudden stops, their cars can spin out of control.

1. ○ sensible
   ○ feeble
   ○ humid
   ○ foul

Road conditions affect how cars move and stop. In bad weather cars may __2__. Some small accidents are known as "fender benders." In a fender bender the people in the cars usually do not get hurt because the cars are not traveling very fast. Most of the time the cars can be driven away without having to be towed, and the damage is __3__. Fender benders are more scary than deadly.

2. ○ volunteer
   ○ collide
   ○ clatter
   ○ romp

3. ○ slight
   ○ plentiful
   ○ lukewarm
   ○ elementary

Unfortunately, accidents may happen even in perfect weather. They may occur if drivers take their minds off their driving even for a moment. Experienced drivers always pay attention to what they are doing. They know how important it is to stay __4__ to other cars around them, to traffic signals, and to people and animals that may be crossing the road. That is why driver's education classes put so much emphasis on caution and safety.

4. ○ tidy
   ○ weary
   ○ alert
   ○ content

5. What might happen if drivers do not pay attention?

_____

6. How would you rate the damage that occurs in a fender bender?

_____

7. What kind of weather can be a problem for drivers?

_____

8. What may happen to cars in bad weather?

_____

Analogies

In each of the following circle the letter for the item that best completes the comparison. Then explain the relationship on the lines provided.

1. sensible is to **foolish** as
   a. eternal is to everlasting
   b. tidy is to messy
   c. accurate is to exact
   d. constant is to continuous

Relationship: _____

_____

_____

_____

3. trudge is to **hurry** as
   a. smolder is to blaze
   b. digest is to absorb
   c. distract is to sidetrack
   d. blossom is to flourish

Relationship: _____

_____

_____

_____

2. feeble is to **weak** as
   a. staple is to unnecessary
   b. worthy is to useless
   c. epidemic is to limited
   d. antique is to ancient

Relationship: _____

_____

_____

4. quiver is to **archer** as
   a. dugout is to pitcher
   b marathon is to runner
   c. backpack is to hiker
   d. medal is to skater

Relationship: _____

_____

_____

Challenge: Make up your own

Write a comparison using the words in the box below. (Hint: There are three possible analogies.) Then write the relationship on the lines provided.

petal	page	grief	scholar
pioneer	disaster	triumph	flower
joy	study	book	explore

Analogy: _____ is to _____ as _____ is to _____.

Relationship: _____

*The words in **boldface** in the sentences below are related to words introduced in Units 5–8. For example, the adjectives* worthless *and* hasty *in item 1 are related to the adjective* worthy *and the noun* haste *(both in Unit 5). Based on your under standing of the unit words, circle the related word in **boldface** that best completes each sentence.*

scholar	humid	distract	envy	noble
content	establish	weary	volunteer	survive
accurate	worthy	antique	penetrate	oppose
reserve	collide	haste	ancestor	disaster

1. Now that the movie theater has closed, the free passes that we won are (**worthless/hasty**).

2. Many people are interested in tracing their (**scholarship/ancestry**) back hundreds of years.

3. There was strong (**opposition/establishment**) when the governor announced new taxes.

4. Scientists predicted the (**collision/weariness**) between a comet and a moon of Jupiter.

5. In the wild, (**accuracy/survival**) depends on an animal's ability to find food, water, and safety.

6. A(n) (**envious/disastrous**) fire burned for days and ruined thousands of acres of forest.

7. Tropical plants and flowers grow best in high (**nobility/humidity**).

8. Adding machines are (**antiquated/voluntary**) compared with today's small, quiet, high-speed calculators.

9. We made a (**penetration/reservation**) for dinner next week at our favorite restaurant.

10. The street noise was such a (**distraction/contentment**) that it was hard to have a simple conversation.

Something is missing! Find and ring the words from Units 5–8 that are hidden in the grid below. Then choose from these words the ones that best complete the sentences that follow. Write the words in the blanks.

D	I	G	E	S	T	X	F	P	R
R	H	L	P	R	D	Z	N	O	D
O	M	O	N	F	E	E	B	L	E
U	Y	D	U	H	M	C	Z	I	N
G	R	I	F	O	U	L	R	C	W
H	L	W	R	P	A	A	L	Y	Z
T	I	D	Y	P	M	T	P	Q	A
Z	E	A	V	O	G	T	T	D	Q
W	A	Q	K	S	H	E	U	Z	L
D	C	L	M	E	P	R	O	M	P

1. "This looks like a case of _____ play," said the detective.

2. "Shush!" said the librarian. "Stop that _____."

3. "Take the puppies outside to _____ and play," said Dad.

4. "Today's rain will bring relief from the long, hot _____," said the weather forecaster.

5. "If you chew your food well, it will be easy to _____," said Mom.

6. "It is our _____ to give a full refund if the item you buy does not work," said the store manager.

CUMULATIVE REVIEW I

 **Definitions**

Choose the word from the box that matches each definition. Write the word on the line provided. The first one has been done for you.

haul	clatter	disaster	constant	~~counsel~~
digest	competition	envy	ambush	humid
indicate	previous	obtain	penetrate	noble
stun	suitable	vanity	weary	yield

1. a lawyer in a legal case   counsel

2. trying to outdo others; a game or contest

3. the product or amount made or produced

4. to understand or grasp an idea

5. loyal, steady, or faithful

6. to want what others have

7. to move by pulling, dragging, or carting

8. coming before in time or order

9. to shock, daze; to make unable to feel, react, or think

10. to pass through, enter, grasp, soak, or see into

11. a hard, rattling sound; noisy chattering

12. the quality of being stuck-up or vain

13. feeling tired, worn out; having no more patience

14. steamy or heavy with moisture; damp

15. to gain or get through some effort

Antonyms

*Choose the word from the box that is most nearly **opposite** in meaning to each group of words. Write the word on the line provided. The first one has been done for you.*

1. an unknown, a nobody   <u>celebrity</u>

2. to expand, enlarge

3. offensive, unappealing

4. courage, excitement

5. modern, new, current, fresh

6. to shrink, wither, fade

7. unimportant, minor, unnecessary

8. to refuse, deny, disallow

9. fair, honest, clean, pure

10. secondary, complex, advanced

11. to splurge, squander, waste

12. a draftee

13. useless, no-good

14. random, irregular, unusual

15. to empower, raise up

16. calm, careful, orderly

17. mistaken, false, misleading

18. flattery, praise, a compliment

19. gentle, tender, kindly

20. fleeting, short, temporary, brief

accurate
antique
attractive
blossom
~~celebrity~~
consent
contract
demonstrate
dread
elementary
essential
eternal
foul
frantic
gallant
humble
pioneer
reserve
routine
slight
sponsor
stern
sturdy
volunteer
worthy

Completing the Sentence

Choose the word from the box that best completes each sentence below. Write the word in the space provided. The first one has been done for you.

Group A

~~contribute~~	thaw	hardship	employ
sincere	urgent	neglect	shabby

1. We decided to _____contribute_____ thirty dollars to the fund for new gym equipment.

2. It is never a _____ to take care of my friend's playful puppy.

3. If you _____ your teeth, you may get cavities, develop sore gums, or even lose a tooth.

4. When we moved to our new house, we replaced our _____ old dining room table.

5. After Monday's cold snap, it took several days for the stream behind our school to _____.

Group B

alert	collide	feeble	haste
oppose	policy	noble	trudge

1. Some people who _____ cruel treatment of animals decide to become vegetarians.

2. Many American students memorize the _____ words of the Declaration of Independence.

3. People in a hurry often eat with such _____ that they end up getting heartburn.

4. Parents should always give a baby-sitter the phone numbers of people to _____ in case of emergency.

5. My dad's company has a _____ that permits employees to wear casual clothing on Fridays.

 **Classifying** *Choose the word from the box that goes best with each group of words. Write the word in the space provided. Then explain what the words have in common. The first one has been done for you.*

annual	baggage	basic	~~calculate~~	dependable
drought	drowsy	lukewarm	quiver	romp

1. estimate, compute, _____calculate_____

   The words name mathematical operations. _____

2. sleepy, sluggish, _____

   _____

3. bow, arrow, _____

   _____

4. hot, _____, cold

   _____

5. daily, weekly, monthly, _____

   _____

6. _____, intermediate, advanced

   _____

7. reliable, responsible, _____

   _____

8. suitcases, trunks, _____

   _____

9. famine, epidemic, plague, _____

   _____

10. stomp, clomp, _____

    _____

Definitions

Study the spelling, pronunciation, part of speech, and definition given for each of the words below. Write the word in the blank space in the sentence that follows. Then read the synonyms and antonyms.

1. **convict**
   (*v.,* kən 'vikt;
   n., 'kän vikt)

   (v.) to prove or judge to be guilty
   The jury voted to _____ the defendant.
   (n.) a person who has been proved guilty of a crime and sentenced to prison; someone who is serving a long prison term
   In a prison a _____ is usually given a job to do.
   SYNONYMS: to condemn, sentence; a prisoner, inmate, felon, criminal
   ANTONYMS: to acquit, free, release

2. **discipline**
   ('di sə plən)

   (n.) punishment; training that results in obedience and self-control; orderly behavior; control gained by enforcing rules of conduct; a branch of knowledge
   Drill instructors insist on strict military _____.
   (v.) to punish; to train in proper behavior; to bring under control
   The principal knows how to _____ rowdy students.
   SYNONYMS: correction, control, direction, drill, practice; to correct, chastise, penalize, subdue, limit
   ANTONYMS: confusion, disorder, rebellion; to forgive

3. **dungeon**
   ('dən jən)

   (n.) a dark room or cell used as a prison, usually underground
   The story described the terror of being locked in a _____.
   SYNONYMS: a keep, hold, hole

4. **earnest**
   ('ər nəst)

   (adj.) serious, important, or grave
   An _____ desire to help others may lead a person to choose a career in medicine.
   SYNONYMS: intent, solemn
   ANTONYMS: insincere, trivial, frivolous, foolish

5. **enclose**
   (in 'klōz)

   (v.) to surround on every side; to close up in or fence off; to include with something else
   Be sure to _____ payment with the bill.
   SYNONYMS: to confine, cage; to cover, encircle, envelop; to include, insert
   ANTONYMS: to release, free; to omit, exclude, leave out

6. **gradual**
   ('gra jə wəl)

   (adj.) happening step-by-step or by degrees; changing little by little
   There may be _____ improvement in a patient's condition after surgery.
   SYNONYMS: moderate, slow, steady
   ANTONYMS: sudden, abrupt

When they are hatched and for the first few months of their lives, birds must rely upon their parents to **nourish** (word 9) them.

7. **grumble**
('grəm bəl)

(v.) to complain angrily but not loudly; to growl
Many people _____ when they have to wait on a long line.
(n.) a growling sound; a muttered complaint
The announcement of the delay brought a _____ from the passengers.
SYNONYMS: to mutter, rumble, mumble; to complain, fuss; a protest

8. **jagged**
('ja gəd)

(adj.) with a rough or sharp edge; irregular or harsh
I cut my hand on a _____ piece of broken glass.
SYNONYMS: ragged, serrated; uneven, rugged
ANTONYMS: smooth, even, regular

9. **nourish**
('nər ish)

(v.) to feed or help grow and develop; to support
A teacher works to _____ a love of learning in students.
SYNONYMS: to nurture, raise, provide for, cherish; to foster, maintain, sustain
ANTONYMS: to starve, neglect, abandon

10. **provision**
(prə 'vi zhən)

(n.) the act of supplying or making available; a stock of food or supplies; a step taken ahead of time; a condition, as in a contract
A good hotel makes every possible _____ for the comfort of its guests.
(v.) to supply with food or materials
It takes tons of food to _____ an army.
SYNONYMS: an arrangement, preparation; a requirement; to furnish, stock

11. **treaty**
('trē tē)

(n.) an agreement or contract between two or more countries, arrived at by discussion and compromise; the legal document that has the terms of such an agreement
The warring nations finally signed a peace _____.
SYNONYMS: a pact, settlement, accord

12. **uneasy**
(ən 'ē zē)

(adj.) feeling worried or unsure; causing discomfort
I often feel _____ before a final exam.
SYNONYMS: troubled, edgy, disturbed, anxious; jittery, nervous, jumpy
ANTONYMS: relaxed, certain, calm, comfortable

For each item below choose the word whose meaning is suggested by the clue given. Then write the word in the space provided.

1. Good _____ teaches a person self-control.
   a. provision   b. dungeon   c. treaty   d. discipline

2. The cage that _____ my parakeet is filled with toys.
   a. nourishes   b. encloses   c. disciplines   d. convicts

3. A written agreement between countries is called a _____.
   a. dungeon   b. discipline   c. treaty   d. convict

4. Someone serious in manner might be described as _____.
   a. jagged   b. gradual   c. uneasy   d. earnest

5. People who feel awkward or nervous may say they are _____.
   a. uneasy   b. gradual   c. earnest   d. jagged

6. A jury will _____ a defendant they believe to be guilty.
   a. nourish   b. convict   c. provision   d. grumble

7. Human hair and fingernails grow at a(n) _____ rate.
   a. gradual   b. earnest   c. jagged   d. uneasy

8. The castle had a dark _____ for captives.
   a. convict   b. provision   c. dungeon   d. treaty

9. If you drop a glass, it will probably break into _____ pieces.
   a. gradual   b. jagged   c. uneasy   d. earnest

10. To complain in a low but angry voice is to _____.
    a. grumble   b. convict   c. enclose   d. nourish

11. Before you go away on vacation, you should make _____ for someone to take care of your pet.
    a. convicts   b. disciplines   c. provisions   d. dungeons

12. Adults help babies to grow and develop by _____ them.
    a. nourishing   b. enclosing   c. disciplining   d. grumbling

Synonyms

*For each item below choose the word that is most nearly the **same** in meaning as the word or phrase in **boldface.** Then write your choice on the line provided.*

1. a **solemn** apology
   a. gradual   b. jagged   c. uneasy   d. earnest   _____

2. alone in the damp **keep**
   a. treaty   b. discipline   c. dungeon   d. provision   _____

3. signed the **pact** for increased trade
   a. treaty   b. convict   c. dungeon   d. grumble   _____

4. **complain** about the weather
   a. grumble   b. convict   c. enclose   d. nourish   _____

5. **confined** the dogs in the yard
   a. disciplined   b. enclosed   c. nourished   d. convicted   _____

6. a **condition** of the contract
   a. treaty   b. dungeon   c. provision   d. convict   _____

Antonyms

*For each item below choose the word that is most nearly **opposite** in meaning to the word or phrase in **boldface.** Then write your choice on the line provided.*

1. the **even** peaks of the mountain range
   a. gradual   b. jagged   c. uneasy   d. earnest   _____

2. came to a **sudden** stop
   a. uneasy   b. earnest   c. jagged   d. gradual   _____

3. **neglected** the growing plants
   a. nourished   b. disciplined   c. provisioned   d. enclosed   _____

4. **freed** the defendant
   a. disciplined   b. nourished   c. convicted   d. provisioned   _____

5. gave us a **relaxed** smile
   a. uneasy   b. earnest   c. gradual   d. jagged   _____

6. **disorder** in the classroom
   a. treaties   b. discipline   c. convicts   d. grumbles   _____

Completing the Sentence

From the list of words on pages 76–77, choose the one that best completes each item below. Then write the word in the space provided. (You may have to change the word's ending.)

A FITTING NICKNAME

■ A frontier town was a rough and often lawless place. There was such a lack of order and _____ that the frontier became know as the "Wild West."

■ Today when people are accused of committing crimes, they get their day in court. But frontier towns did not always bother with a judge and jury. Angry mobs or enemies out for revenge often _____ people on the spot.

■ In an attempt to bring some order to life, many towns enacted _____ that required people to leave their weapons with the sheriff when they came to town.

■ There were complaints, but the system led to a(n) _____ peace. People still could not feel sure that they were safe.

■ Law and order did not come overnight; but settlers did see a(n) _____ improvement in law enforcement.

TEARS WITHOUT TEARS

■ If you accidentally tear a dollar bill in half, your first reaction may be to _____ or cry. But all is not lost!

■ Don't bother trying to tape, paste, or staple the _____ edges of the bill back together.

■ Just _____ the pieces in an envelope and take them to a bank. A teller will give you a new bill in exchange for the torn one.

FAIR CARE

■ International _____ state that prisoners of war must receive decent and humane treatment at the hands of their captors.

■ Whether they are held in damp _____ or modern jails, prisoners must be given food, water, and basic medical care.

■ Some may be allowed to read or write to _____ their minds and spirits.

■ Unfortunately, some nations have not made a(n) _____ effort to treat prisoners decently. A number of human rights groups work hard to force these nations to take these rules seriously.

 Circle the letter next to the word or expression that best completes the sentence or answers the question. Pay special attention to the word in **boldface.**

1. A teacher who demands strict **discipline** might say
   a. "Shall we start math now?"
   b. "Let's skip spelling today."
   c. "Raise your hand to talk."
   d. "Chat all you want today."

2. Which of these is **jagged**?
   a. a bowl of spaghetti
   b. a baseball cap
   c. a ball of yarn
   d. a saw blade

3. It's likely a **dungeon** would be
   a. warm and fuzzy
   b. hot and humid
   c. cozy and homey
   d. dark and damp

4. You know I feel **uneasy** because
   a. I smile all the time
   b. I stand up straight
   c. my clothes are new
   d. my hands are shaking

5. **Earnest** students would
   a. pay attention in class
   b. not care about school
   c. walk to school
   d. sleep in class

6. Which would **nourish** a kitten?
   a. a big dog
   b. a bowl of milk
   c. a catnip toy
   d. a flea collar

7. Which best **encloses** a yard?
   a. a stream
   b. a highway
   c. a fence
   d. a cage

8. Lunch **provisions** may include
   a. hungry people
   b. posters about good health
   c. bread for sandwiches
   d. tubes of toothpaste

9. If **convicts** get away, they escape
   a. from the scene of a crime
   b. from kitchen chores
   c. from jail
   d. from the circus

10. When I **grumble**, I
    a. do my homework
    b. complain a lot
    c. raise my voice
    d. go to the movies

11. Two nations sign a **treaty** if
    a. they both agree
    b. they both want a party
    c. they both raise taxes
    d. both go to war

12. During a **gradual** warming spell, temperatures may go
    a. from 65° F to 25° F
    b. from 65° F to 67° F
    c. from 65° F to 99° F
    d. from 65° F to 55° F

Definitions

Study the spelling, pronunciation, part of speech, and definition given for each of the words below. Write the word in the blank space in the sentence that follows. Then read the synonyms and antonyms.

1. **distress**
   (di 'stres)

   (n.) deep worry or suffering; being in danger or in trouble
   The Coast Guard helps boats in _____.

   (v.) to trouble or upset; to cause worry or stress; to make unhappy
   Our dogs, who bark at every noise, may _____ our sick neighbor.

   SYNONYMS: anguish, anxiety, grief, torment; to upset, bother, disturb, irritate
   ANTONYMS: calm, joy, delight; to calm, gladden, comfort, soothe

2. **drench**
   (drench)

   (v.) to wet or soak through and through; to cover or fill completely
   A night of rain is enough to _____ the field.

   SYNONYMS: to saturate, flood, douse, sop, drown
   ANTONYMS: to dry, parch

3. **dwell**
   (dwel)

   (v.) to live, especially in a particular place; to remain, stay; to keep one's attention on something
   Do you think that human beings will one day _____ on the moon?

   SYNONYMS: to inhabit, reside; to linger, last

4. **juvenile**
   ('jü və nīl)

   (adj.) not fully grown; of or meant for children or young people; foolish or immature
   His _____ pranks are so annoying!

   (n.) a young person or individual
   The play has a big part for a _____.

   SYNONYMS: young, youthful, childish; a youth, minor
   ANTONYMS: mature, developed; an adult

5. **outstanding**
   (aut 'stan diŋ)

   (adj.) standing apart from others due to being excellent; unpaid
   The firefighter was praised for her _____ bravery.

   SYNONYMS: remarkable, great, noteworthy, unusual, superior; unpaid
   ANTONYMS: ordinary, regular, usual, average

6. **proceed**
   (prō 'sēd)

   (v.) to go on or continue in an orderly way; to start again after a pause; to start an action, move
   We must _____ directly to a hospital.

   SYNONYMS: to advance, progress
   ANTONYMS: to recede, retreat, stand, stay, stop

Helicopters can help people in **distress** (word 1) in areas that are difficult or impossible to reach with rescue vehicles.

7. **register**
('re je stər)

(n.) an official record book; the range of a voice or musical instrument; a machine that records data
How many names are on the class _____?

(v.) to sign up; to show on a scale; to note or understand
When must we _____ *for Little League?*

SYNONYMS: a roster, catalog, ledger; to enroll, enlist, join; to express, demonstrate
ANTONYMS: to withdraw

8. **sift**
(sift)

(v.) to put through a strainer to separate or break up lumps; to sort through or examine
It took some time to _____ *through all the mail.*

SYNONYMS: to separate, strain, filter, screen; to examine, study

9. **spree**
(sprē)

(n.) a lively or wild outburst of activity
The prize was a thirty-minute shopping _____.

SYNONYMS: a riot, binge, bash, fling, splurge

10. **tardy**
('tär dē)

(adj.) not on time, delayed; slow-moving
Have you ever been _____ *for school?*

SYNONYMS: late, overdue; sluggish
ANTONYMS: early, prompt

11. **unfit**
(ən 'fit)

(adj.) not suitable or proper; not good enough; unhealthy
The flood made tap water _____ *to drink.*

SYNONYMS: bad, improper, inappropriate, inadequate, unqualified; incompetent
ANTONYMS: suitable, proper, appropriate, qualified; healthy, fit, sound

12. **variety**
(və 'rī tē)

(n.) change, lack of sameness; a number of different forms or types; a category of plants or animals
The old saying has it that " _____ *is the spice of life."*

SYNONYMS: diversity, difference; an assortment, selection
ANTONYMS: sameness, unity

Match the Meaning

For each item below choose the word whose meaning is suggested by the clue given. Then write the word in the space provided.

1. In most stores you will find a cash _____.
   a. distress b. spree c. variety d. register

2. To soak something with water is to _____ it.
   a. proceed b. drench c. register d. sift

3. Eat a _____ of foods to avoid boring meals.
   a. spree b. register c. variety d. distress

4. An _____ book is one that is much better than most.
   a. unfit b. tardy c. juvenile d. outstanding

5. To live in a particular place is to _____ there.
   a. dwell b. drench c. sift d. distress

6. One who suffers great pain is in _____.
   a. register b. distress c. juvenile d. variety

7. If I'm not on time, I'm _____.
   a. tardy b. outstanding c. unfit d. juvenile

8. A lively outburst of activity is a _____.
   a. distress b. register c. spree d. variety

9. Spoiled food is _____ to eat.
   a. tardy b. unfit c. juvenile d. outstanding

10. People _____ soil to break apart lumps.
    a. sift b. distress c. drench d. register

11. A book meant for young people might be described as _____.
    a. outstanding b. unfit c. juvenile d. tardy

12. Football games _____ in almost any weather.
    a. proceed b. drench c. register d. distress

Synonyms

*For each item below choose the word that is most nearly the **same** in meaning as the word or phrase in **boldface**. Then write your choice on the line provided.*

1. a memory that **lingers**
   a. registers   b. dwells   c. distresses   d. drenches   _____

2. a berry-eating **binge**
   a. distress   b. variety   c. juvenile   d. spree   _____

3. the wide **assortment** of colors
   a. variety   b. distress   c. spree   d. register   _____

4. **scatter** cinnamon into the batter
   a. sift   b. distress   c. drench   d. proceed   _____

5. to **saturate** the paper
   a. register   b. drench   c. proceed   d. sift   _____

6. the latest **roster** of players
   a. spree   b. distress   c. register   d. juvenile   _____

Antonyms

*For each item below choose the word that is most nearly **opposite** in meaning to the word or phrase in **boldface**. Then write your choice on the line provided.*

1. **qualified** to run a marathon
   a. tardy   b. unfit   c. juvenile   d. outstanding _____

2. is known for being **prompt**
   a. juvenile   b. tardy   c. unfit   d. outstanding _____

3. **average** strength
   a. juvenile   b. tardy   c. outstanding   d. unfit   _____

4. **mature** sense of humor
   a. unfit   b. outstanding   c. juvenile   d. tardy   _____

5. decided to **retreat**
   a. proceed   b. register   c. sift   d. drench   _____

6. to **comfort** the children
   a. distress   b. proceed   c. register   d. drench   _____

Completing the Sentence

From the list of words on pages 82–83, choose the one that best completes each item below. Then write the word in the space provided. (You may have to change the word's ending.)

AN APPLE A DAY

■ There are many _____ of apples available today. You can usually find four or five kinds in the local supermarket.

■ The McIntosh is a(n) _____ apple to eat raw—one of the finest—but it turns to mush when you cook it.

■ Bruised apples may be _____ to serve fresh, but they are perfectly suitable for making tasty applesauce.

HOW TO LOSE A RACE

■ We were supposed to _____ by noon on Saturday for the big bicycle race.

■ We planned to enter the _____ division, which was for kids under thirteen.

■ But we got involved in a Saturday morning cartoon _____, and we lost track of time.

■ That's often what happens when you _____ in front of a television.

■ When we got to the park at 12:30 P.M., we found that we were too _____ to sign up. We had only ourselves to blame for being so late.

LIBRARY EMERGENCY

■ Yesterday the fire station got a _____ call from the public library. There was some kind of trouble there.

■ A crew _____ quickly to the building, expecting to see flames and smoke.

■ Instead they found hundreds of books _____ with water from a broken pipe.

■ Worried librarians _____ through the mess to find any books they could save. Fortunately some of the books on the bottom shelves were still dry.

Word Associations

*Circle the letter next to the word or expression that best completes the sentence or answers the question. Pay special attention to the word in **boldface**.*

1. In a **register** you might find
   a. shoes
   b. records
   c. gloves
   d. sandwiches

2. Milk is **unfit** to drink if it is
   a. cold
   b. expensive
   c. sour
   d. flavored

3. If I'm **tardy**, I might be told
   a. "You're early!"
   b. "You're lost!"
   c. "Thank you."
   d. "You're late!"

4. Which is a **juvenile**?
   a. a grandmother
   b. a newly hatched chick
   c. a police officer
   d. a car seat

5. You might come back from a **spree**
   a. with a lot of packages
   b. with chicken pox
   c. with a haircut
   d. with a snack

6. Which might you **sift**?
   a. flour
   b. relatives
   c. homework
   d. movies

7. At a camp that offers a **variety** of sports, you might
   a. swim, wrestle, and skate
   b. only play volleyball
   c. meet a famous gymnast
   d. get the same food every day

8. Where do bears **dwell**?
   a. in the ocean
   b. in the sky
   c. in a forest
   d. in apartments

9. If you have **outstanding** bills,
   a. you are remarkable
   b. you owe money
   c. you never sit
   d. you dislike being inside

10. If the action **proceeds**,
    a. it stops
    b. it makes you laugh
    c. it makes you cry
    d. it goes on

11. You're **drenched** in jewelry if you
    a. are extremely thirsty
    b. wear many bracelets and rings
    c. are a swimmer
    d. wear dark sunglasses

12. For a friend in **distress**, you'd
    a. probably jump for joy
    b. probably offer help
    c. probably order lunch
    d. probably change your clothes

Definitions

Study the spelling, pronunciation, part of speech, and definition given for each of the words below. Write the word in the blank space in the sentence that follows. Then read the synonyms and antonyms.

1. **blockade**
   (blä 'kād)

   (v.) to close off or keep people or supplies from going in or out
   Warships may be used to _____ a harbor.

   (n.) the closing off of an enemy nation, city, port, or area, usually by the military; something that closes off or keeps out
   During the Civil War, the Union forces used a land and sea _____ to cut off the city of Charleston, South Carolina.

   SYNONYMS: to besiege, isolate, obstruct; a siege; a barrier
   ANTONYMS: to open; an opening

2. **chant**
   (chant)

   (v.) to sing; to recite in a tone that varies only a little or not at all
   Let us _____ the ancient poems together.

   (n.) a song in such a tone; words or phrases repeated in rhythm
   At a soccer match the _____ of thousands of fans excites the teams to do their best.

   SYNONYMS: to intone, vocalize; a hymn, incantation, singsong, recitation

3. **despair**
   (di 'spâr)

   (v.) to give up all hope, lose heart
   We _____ of ever seeing them again.

   (n.) total loss of hope; a cause of loss of hope
   If fear changes to _____, a person might give up trying.

   SYNONYMS: hopelessness, dismay, discouragement
   ANTONYMS: to hope, encourage, take heart; hopefulness, cheer, confidence

4. **elevate**
   ('e lə vāt)

   (v.) to raise or lift up; to increase in position or rank; to cheer up; to improve culturally, intellectually, or morally
   If your foot is swollen, your doctor may tell you to _____ it.

   SYNONYMS: to boost, heighten, hoist; to advance, promote, upgrade
   ANTONYMS: to lower, drop, lessen; to disgrace, demote

5. **extraordinary**
   (ik 'strôr dən er ē)

   (adj.) beyond the usual or expected; highly unusual or rare
   My best friend has an _____ singing voice.

   SYNONYMS: great, exceptional, amazing, remarkable
   ANTONYMS: ordinary, usual, average, run-of-the-mill

6. **heroic**
   (hi 'rō ik)

   (adj.) brave, noble, or larger than life; involving extreme effort
   Many poems have been written about the _____ deeds of ancient warriors.

   SYNONYMS: courageous, bold, fearless, gallant
   ANTONYMS: cowardly; minimal, trivial

Children often use **chants** (word 2) to help them keep time when they jump rope.

7. **lance**
(lans)

(n.) a long, metal-tipped weapon used by knights or soldiers on horseback; any sharp, pointed instrument that resembles such a weapon
In the Middle Ages, each knight carried a _____ into battle.
(v.) to pierce with or as if with a lance; to open a wound
A doctor may decide to _____ an infected blister.
SYNONYMS: a spear, shaft; to puncture, cut, cut open

8. **missionary**
('mi shə ner ē)

(n.) a person on an assignment, often of a religious nature; someone sent by a church to a foreign land to teach religion and do charity work
The life of a _____ requires courage and dedication.
(adj.) related to or involved with such an assignment
The peacekeepers worked with a _____ spirit.
SYNONYM: a preacher

9. **pointless**
('point ləs)

(adj.) having no meaning or effect
Sometimes it is _____ to continue a conversation.
SYNONYMS: senseless, aimless, futile, meaningless, worthless, ineffective, unproductive
ANTONYMS: fitting, meaningful, sensible, effective, valuable

10. **reflect**
(ri 'flekt)

(v.) to throw back, as heat, light, or sound; to give back an image of, as a mirror; to make apparent, show, or demonstrate; to think deeply about
The surface of the lake will _____ the clouds in the sky.
SYNONYMS: to mirror, copy, echo, return; to reveal; to consider, ponder, muse
ANTONYMS: to absorb, retain; to disregard, ignore

11. **site**
(sīt)

(n.) a location, scene, or place where something was, is, or will be
Yorktown was the _____ of a famous battle.
SYNONYMS: a spot, location, position

12. **toxic**
('täk sik)

(adj.) poisonous or deadly
A gas mask can filter out _____ fumes.
SYNONYMS: dangerous, harmful, venomous, lethal
ANTONYMS: nontoxic, safe, harmless

Match the Meaning

For each item below choose the word whose meaning is suggested by the clue given. Then write the word in the space provided.

1. A cartoon superhero usually has _____ powers.
   a. pointless   b. toxic   c. missionary   d. extraordinary

2. In wartime a country may use a _____ to keep supplies from reaching the enemy.
   a. missionary   b. chant   c. lance   d. blockade

3. To increase a person's rank or position is to _____ that person.
   a. reflect   b. elevate   c. blockade   d. chant

4. A _____ is a long spear with a metal point.
   a. site   b. blockade   c. lance   d. missionary

5. If you lose heart when things go badly, you _____.
   a. reflect   b. chant   c. despair   d. lance

6. A brave person whose actions seem larger than life is a _____ individual.
   a. heroic   b. missionary   c. pointless   d. toxic

7. Mother Theresa was a famous _____ who helped the poor.
   a. blockade   b. missionary   c. chant   d. site

8. The place where a home is built is called its _____.
   a. despair   b. chant   c. site   d. missionary

9. A(n) _____ remark is one that has no meaning.
   a. heroic   b. pointless   c. missionary   d. extraordinary

10. A song or hymn that is mostly in the same tone is called a _____.
    a. blockade   b. site   c. lance   d. chant

11. Something that is poisonous may be described as _____.
    a. missionary   b. pointless   c. toxic   d. heroic

12. When a surface gives back an image, it is said to _____ that image.
    a. reflect   b. elevate   c. blockade   d. despair

Synonyms

*For each item below choose the word that is most nearly the **same** in meaning as the word or phrase in **boldface**. Then write your choice on the line provided.*

1. discovered some **exceptional** fossils
   a. toxic   b. pointless   c. extraordinary d. missionary _____

2. found the best **spot** for our picnic
   a. chant   b. missionary c. lance   d. site   _____

3. after the doctor **punctures** the wound
   a. reflects b. lances   c. elevates d. blockades _____

4. the monks' recording of **hymns**
   a. chants   b. lances   c. blockades d. sites   _____

5. ordered the troops to **isolate** the enemy town
   a. lance   b. despair   c. blockade d. reflect _____

6. chose to work as a **preacher**
   a. blockade b. missionary c. lance   d. site   _____

Antonyms

*For each item below choose the word that is most nearly **opposite** in meaning to the word or phrase in **boldface**. Then write your choice on the line provided.*

1. a **meaningful** action
   a. heroic   b. pointless   c. toxic d. extraordinary _____

2. a medicine that **lowers** blood pressure
   a. elevates b. blockades c. chants   d. reflects _____

3. remembered for their **cowardly** deeds
   a. missionary b. toxic   c. pointless d. heroic   _____

4. **harmless** to pets
   a. pointless b. heroic   c. toxic   d. reflected _____

5. materials that **absorb** sound
   a. reflect   b. blockade c. chant   d. elevate _____

6. a story of **faith**
   a. blockade b. chant   c. despair   d. site   _____

Completing the Sentence

From the list of words on pages 88–89, choose the one that best completes each item below. Then write the word in the space provided. (You may have to change the word's ending.)

FIRST AID FIRST!

■ One of the dangers of hiking or camping is snake bite. If you are bitten, it is _____ to panic. There is nothing to be gained by going to pieces.

■ You need not _____ if you can stay calm. Rather than lose hope, the important thing is to take some simple first-aid steps.

■ Tie off the bite to keep _____ fluids from traveling through your body.

■ If swelling occurs, you may have to _____ the bite with a clean, sharp knife. Then go immediately to the nearest doctor or hospital.

SPECIAL REWARDS

■ People who choose the life of a _____ need to be strong and brave. Their choice can bring many difficulties and hardships. But it can also bring them remarkable experiences and special rewards.

■ They may travel to _____ places that few outsiders have ever visited. They may meet people who are very different from themselves.

■ The good works of these dedicated individuals _____ their wish to help others. Such a life can enrich both the helpers and those they help.

CIVIL RIGHTS FOR ALL

■ There are times when bold acts by ordinary people _____ us all to new heights of justice.

■ Before the civil rights movement of the 1960s, some people set up _____ to keep blacks from entering "white" schools and stores.

■ Groups that wanted to end racism got together to _____ sayings such as "We Shall Overcome" and "Equality Now." These people came from all walks of life, but they had the same goal: equal rights for all.

■ Lunch counters, bus stops, and schools were among the _____ of early civil rights struggles.

■ Thanks to the _____ work of African American leaders such as Dr. Martin Luther King, Jr., and of thousands of ordinary people, racial segregation was finally outlawed.

*Circle the letter next to the word or expression that best completes the sentence or answers the question. Pay special attention to the word in **boldface.***

1. A **pointless** movie would be
   a. extremely dull
   b. very long
   c. a little bit funny
   d. without meaning

2. If you make a **heroic** effort, you
   a. try everything you can
   b. think about helping
   c. give up hope
   d. wear a cape or a mask

3. If you drank a **toxic** liquid, you might
   a. sing off-key
   b. grow too big
   c. get very sick
   d. develop superhuman powers

4. The way to **lance** something is
   a. to tickle it
   b. to soak it
   c. to puncture it
   d. to ignore it

5. What might a **missionary** be likely to do?
   a. build a church
   b. read gossip magazines
   c. move to Antarctica
   d. ignore other people

6. With **extraordinary** speed, you
   a. would win most races
   b. would love to read
   c. would walk a lot
   d. would sleep late

7. If a pond **reflects** the trees around it, you can
   a. throw sticks into the water
   b. see the trees in the water
   c. throw away your mirror
   d. think about nature

8. To **elevate** your hand,
   a. hold it over your head
   b. put it in your pocket
   c. shake it back and forth
   d. wear a mitten

9. When I moved away, I **despaired**
   a. of getting any birthday cards
   b. of seeing my old friends
   c. of having enough food
   d. of finding a movie theater

10. You might **chant** if you like to
    a. take risks
    b. sing
    c. exercise
    d. watch television

11. Which is a historic **site**?
    a. President Lincoln's top hat
    b. the Stars and Stripes
    c. the White House
    d. the U.S. Constitution

12. Which might form a **blockade**?
    a. trays of ice cubes
    b. boards and bricks
    c. first-aid kits
    d. pens and pencils

Definitions

Study the spelling, pronunciation, part of speech, and definition given for each of the words below. Write the word in the blank space in the sentence that follows. Then read the synonyms and antonyms.

1. **bristle**
('bri səl)

(n.) a stiff, short hair or fiber
Use a toothbrush with soft, gentle _____.
(v.) to have hair standing on end; to show anger; to be full of
An insulting remark may make a person _____ with anger.
SYNONYMS: a whisker, spine, quill; to stiffen, rise, seethe, teem, swarm

2. **circular**
('sər kyə lər)

(adj.) forming, moving, or being like a circle, round; indirect
The _____ pathway goes around the pond.
(n.) a leaflet or printed advertisement meant to be given to many people
We received a _____ describing sales at the mall.
SYNONYMS: ring-shaped, disc-shaped; roundabout; flyer, handbill, brochure
ANTONYMS: linear, straight, direct

3. **coarse**
(kôrs)

(adj.) low, common, or of poor quality; made of comparatively large parts; rough to the touch; using bad manners or rude language
Most people are offended by _____ behavior.
SYNONYMS: rugged, crude, harsh, grainy; scratchy; vulgar, foul, gross
ANTONYMS: smooth, silky, delicate; gentle, refined, polite

4. **discard**
(*v.,* dis 'kärd;
n., 'dis kärd)

(v.) to get rid of or throw away
Please _____ your newspapers into recycling bins.
(n.) something cast off or thrown away
Donate your clothing _____ to a charity.
SYNONYMS: to dump, dispose of, eliminate
ANTONYMS: to save, keep, retain

5. **extreme**
(ik 'strēm)

(adj.) to the highest or greatest degree; exaggerated; farthest possible
Most people avoid _____ heat and cold.
(n.) the highest, farthest, or greatest; one end of a range
Songs often describe _____ of emotion.
SYNONYMS: utmost, ultimate; excessive, drastic; outermost
ANTONYMS: limited, mild, ordinary, usual; close, near

6. **focus**
('fō kəs)

(n.) sharpness or clarity; the center of activity or interest
It is easy to adjust the _____ of binoculars.
(v.) to correct for sharpness and clarity; to concentrate
Always take the time to _____ your camera.
SYNONYMS: the center, heart, emphasis, direction; to direct, adjust, sharpen
ANTONYMS: the background; to blur, ignore, neglect

7. **grasp**
(grasp)

(v.) to take hold with the arms or hands; to take eagerly; to understand
A person who trips on a stairway will probably _____ the handrail.

(n.) the reach of arms or hands; the power to reach or hold onto; understanding
It's important to have a good _____ of addition.

SYNONYMS: to clutch; to get; to perceive; control; perception, comprehension
ANTONYMS: to drop, release, loosen, free, slip; to misunderstand

8. **inspire**
(in 'spīr)

(v.) to guide, excite, uplift, or encourage; to bring about or cause
The Olympic Games _____ athletes to do their best.

SYNONYMS: to influence, motivate, move, affect, touch, arouse, kindle, spark
ANTONYMS: to deter, discourage

9. **magnify**
('mag nə fī)

(v.) to increase in importance, exaggerate; to make bigger
A microscope can _____ tiny objects.

SYNONYMS: to intensify, increase, inflate, boost; to enlarge, expand, swell
ANTONYMS: to diminish, reduce, lessen, shrink

10. **marine**
(mə 'rēn)

(adj.) related to or of the sea, sailing, or shipping; related to the seagoing branch of the armed forces
Whales are _____ mammals, not fish.

(n.) a soldier who serves on a ship, a member of the U. S. Marine Corps
_____ have taken part in every important American naval battle since 1775.

SYNONYMS: nautical, maritime, oceanic, aquatic, coastal, naval
ANTONYMS: freshwater, land

11. **quake**
(kwāk)

(v.) to shake or move back and forth; to tremble
People who live in California often feel the ground _____.

(n.) a shaking back and forth or trembling; an earthquake
A minor _____ does little damage.

SYNONYMS: to shudder, shiver, vibrate, quaver; a tremor, shock

12. **troublesome**
('trə bəl səm)

(adj.) difficult; causing annoyance, bother, or worry
It is _____ to run out of gas on the highway.

SYNONYMS: hard; annoying, worrisome, bothersome, upsetting
ANTONYMS: easy; untroubling

Match the Meaning

For each item below choose the word whose meaning is suggested by the clue given. Then write the word in the space provided.

1. When a cat crosses a dog's path, the dog's hair may _____.
   a. inspire   b. focus   c. grasp   d. bristle

2. A teacher tries to encourage students and _____ them to study hard.
   a. quake   b. inspire   c. bristle   d. magnify

3. If you take hold of something eagerly, you _____ it.
   a. magnify   b. focus   c. grasp   d. discard

4. Silk feels smooth, but a rough fabric like burlap is _____ to the touch.
   a. troublesome   b. extreme   c. circular   d. coarse

5. CDs, frisbees, and doughnuts are _____ in shape.
   a. circular   b. troublesome   c. coarse   d. marine

6. When you concentrate all your attention on something, you _____ on it.
   a. magnify   b. focus   c. grasp   d. discard

7. A VCR that is hard to use and that ruins tapes could be described as _____.
   a. troublesome   b. circular   c. marine   d. coarse

8. When the ground shakes or moves back and forth, it may be a _____.
   a. focus   b. discard   c. quake   d. bristle

9. Creatures that live in the ocean are _____ animals.
   a. circular   b. marine   c. extreme   d. troublesome

10. When you get rid of things you can no longer use, you _____ them.
    a. discard   b. focus   c. grasp   d. magnify

11. The very severe cold of the Antarctic winter is the most _____ on Earth.
    a. coarse   b. marine   c. extreme   d. circular

12. If you make a mistake seem more serious than it is, you _____ the problem.
    a. discard   b. inspire   c. bristle   d. magnify

Synonyms

*For each item below choose the word that is most nearly the **same** in meaning as the word or phrase in **boldface**. Then write your choice on the line provided.*

1. **shiver** in the cold wind
   a. discard   b. magnify   c. grasp   d. quake   _____

2. a very **difficult** situation
   a. coarse   b. circular   c. marine   d. troublesome   _____

3. **sharpened** the image on the screen
   a. inspired   b. bristled   c. discarded   d. focused   _____

4. **aroused** great loyalty among the players
   a. bristled   b. inspired   c. magnified   d. discarded   _____

5. covered with stiff **hairs**
   a. grasps   b. circulars   c. bristles   d. quakes   _____

6. my favorite **aquatic** sport
   a. marine   b. circular   c. coarse   d. troublesome   _____

Antonyms

*For each item below choose the word that is most nearly **opposite** in meaning to the word or phrase in **boldface**. Then write your choice on the line provided.*

1. **save** your ticket stub
   a. discard   b. inspire   c. magnify   d. focus   _____

2. a **polite** remark
   a. circular   b. marine   c. coarse   d. extreme   _____

3. a **mild** winter
   a. coarse   b. extreme   c. circular   d. troublesome   _____

4. tried to **reduce** the noise
   a. magnify   b. bristle   c. grasp   d. inspire   _____

5. follow the **straight** path
   a. marine   b. extreme   c. coarse   d. circular   _____

6. **misunderstand** the main idea
   a. inspire   b. grasp   c. discard   d. quake   _____

Completing the Sentence

From the list of words on pages 94–95, choose the one that best completes each item below. Then write the word in the space provided. (You may have to change the word's ending.)

From the list of words on pages 94–95

BUYER BEWARE

■ Advertisers try to _____ people to buy their products. They do this by making whatever they have to sell sound appealing and necessary.

■ One way that they do this is through smart, funny ads that _____ your attention on a product and make you want to try it.

■ Some advertisers mail out catalogs or _____ to attract customers. Many people read such ads carefully to find the best bargains.

■ But mail ads do not interest everyone. Some people think of them as junk mail and _____ them without even looking at them.

■ Whatever kind of ads you look at, remember that advertisers may _____ their products' good points. There is plenty of truth to the old saying "Let the buyer beware."

SEEING BENEATH THE SURFACE

■ Snorkeling will do more than give you a close look at all kinds of interesting _____ life. It will give you an idea of what a fish sees.

■ Many colorful fish live near coral reefs. When you snorkel near a reef, you need to use _____ care. Reefs are filled with living creatures, and you must avoid injuring them in any way.

■ You also need to take care that you are not injured by the corals. Many have _____ surfaces that can give you a nasty scrape or cut. And some kinds of corals can sting. So be cautious when snorkeling.

YOU CAN WORK IT OUT

■ You can often solve _____ problems if you talk things out with members of your family or with friends.

■ Don't _____ at the idea of talking about difficult or embarrassing matters. There is really nothing to make you tremble.

■ If another person can _____ what it is that is bothering you, you can work together to find a solution.

■ If you don't agree with what the other person suggests, try not to get angry and _____. Explain what it is you disagree with, and keep talking.

*Circle the letter next to the word or expression that best completes the sentence or answers the question. Pay special attention to the word in **boldface**.*

1. **Extreme** behavior is usually
   a. excessive
   b. friendly
   c. thoughtful
   d. ordinary

2. **Troublesome** neighbors probably
   a. live across the street
   b. annoy you quite often
   c. get a lot of mail
   d. work on weekends

3. Clever inventions **inspire** me
   a. to try to build things myself
   b. to stay inside
   c. to feed the cat
   d. to get a flu shot

4. If you **grasp** a pillow, you
   a. sleep on it
   b. sew a cover for it
   c. put your arms around it
   d. store it in the attic

5. Clocks with **circular** faces
   a. look round
   b. are colorful
   c. look square
   d. are electric

6. A mirror that **magnifies** things makes them look
   a. shinier than they are
   b. flatter than they are
   c. smaller than they are
   d. bigger than they are

7. If you lived through a **quake**, you could describe how
   a. ducks stayed dry
   b. you made a quilt
   c. Earth looked to astronauts
   d. objects shook and moved

8. A hairbrush with soft **bristles**
   a. is good to paint with
   b. is too heavy to lift
   c. is too expensive
   d. is gentle on the scalp

9. If I **focus** on my homework, I
   a. can have two desserts
   b. can get a new camera
   c. can understand the lesson
   d. can play the flute

10. Which is a **marine** animal?
    a. a shark
    b. a tiger
    c. a butterfly
    d. a giraffe

11. A suit of **coarse** cloth feels
    a. silky
    b. scratchy
    c. slimy
    d. smelly

12. If I **discard** a book, I
    a. write an essay on it
    b. read it again
    c. give it away
    d. write my name in it

Selecting Word Meanings

*For each of the following items circle the choice that is most nearly the **same** in meaning as the word in **boldface**.*

1. **blockade** the entry to the fort
   a. close off   b. open up   c. fill in   d. pass by

2. **discipline** the puppy
   a. forgive   b. reward   c. train   d. feed

3. **enclose** a check
   a. spend   b. open   c. cash   d. include

4. **coarse** words
   a. gentle   b. rude   c. fine   d. hoarse

5. within our **grasp**
   a. prison   b. reach   c. neighborhood   d. closet

6. a **pointless** joke
   a. meaningless   b. sensible   c. dull   d. pleasant

7. **dwell** in large groups
   a. play   b. travel   c. leave   d. live

8. a drop in **juvenile** crime
   a. adult   b. organized   c. youthful   d. violent

9. the **site** of the old barn
   a. owner   b. entrance   c. location   d. picture

10. **gradual** deepening of the water
    a. slow   b. sudden   c. dangerous   d. widespread

11. in **extreme** danger
    a. little   b. utmost   c. ordinary   d. some

12. **register** for the contest
    a. practice   b. withdraw   c. referee   d. sign up

Spelling

For each item below study the **boldface** word in which there is a blank. If a letter is missing, fill in the blank to make a correctly spelled word. If the word is already spelled correctly, leave the blank empty.

1. in deep **d__spair**

2. an **outs__anding** student

3. **toxi__** chemicals

4. **proceed__** to the exit

5. **tre__ty** on global warming

6. **unea__y** about the visit

7. **di__card** the envelope

8. **e__rnest** words

9. a **jag__ed** blade

10. **missi__nary** work

11. emergency **provi__ions**

12. **reflec__t** on the past

Antonyms

For each of the following items circle the choice that is most nearly the **opposite** in meaning to the word in **boldface**.

1. decided to **convict** him
   a. sentence   b. judge   c. release   d. arrest

2. **extraordinary** deeds
   a. usual   b. kind   c. amazing   d. cruel

3. **unfit** for the job
   a. unqualified   b. eager   c. available   d. suitable

4. **nourishes** their hopes
   a. feeds   b. starves   c. shares   d. punishes

5. **elevate** our spirits
   a. tease   b. boost   c. require   d. lower

6. a **circular** route
   a. straight   b. roundabout   c. correct   d. unfamiliar

7. hear **distress** in her voice
   a. irritation   b. delight   c. grief   d. doubt

8. **troublesome** chores
   a. annoying   b. thankless   c. easy   d. endless

Vocabulary in Context

Words have been left out of the following passage. For each numbered item in the passage, fill in the circle next to the word in the margin that best fills the blank space. Then answer each question below by writing a sentence that contains one of the words you have chosen.

You have probably watched a wide __1__ of nature shows. You may have seen a plant burst into bloom or watched the slow struggle of a baby snake breaking out of its leathery egg. If you have seen such things, you have experienced the wonder of time-lapse photography.

Most of us notice big changes, but we often miss small ones. Time-lapse photography captures a(n) __2__ process that happens little by little over hours or days. Few of us would have the patience to sit still long enough to observe what a camera can record.

Time-lapse photographers __3__ a camera on one spot for many hours. They may take thousands of hours of film or videotape. During editing, they piece together the most dramatic shots and cut the ones where not much happens. The result seems to speed up time.

Choosing the right __4__ for the camera is as important for time-lapse photographers as choosing a subject. The subject will determine where the camera should be located. For a film about a storm, for example, the camera will be aimed at the wide sky. Once the camera is in place, it will record the story as it unfolds.

1. ○ grasp
   ○ variety
   ○ provision
   ○ blockade

2. ○ extreme
   ○ heroic
   ○ pointless
   ○ gradual

3. ○ sift
   ○ reflect
   ○ focus
   ○ enclose

4. ○ site
   ○ treaty
   ○ register
   ○ lance

5. What do the photographers look for when deciding where to shoot a time-lapse film?

_____

6. Why does time-lapse photography take place over a long time?

_____

7. How do the photographers record this process?

_____

8. How might you see examples of time-lapse photography?

_____

Analogies

In each of the following circle the letter for the item that best completes the comparison. Then explain the relationship on the lines provided.

1. juvenile is to **mature** as
   a. cowardly is to heroic
   b. earnest is to solemn
   c. fast is to quick
   d. tardy is to late

Relationship: _____

_____

_____

_____

3. dungeon is to **prison** as
   a. dark is to light
   b. blockade is to barrier
   c. convict is to jailer
   d. despair is to hope

Relationship: _____

_____

_____

_____

2. chant is to **hymn** as
   a. discipline is to disorder
   b. marine is to civilian
   c. grumble is to protest
   d. variety is to unity

Relationship: _____

_____

_____

_____

4. bristle is to **stiff** as
   a. pillow is to hard
   b. glass is to soft
   c. sandpaper is to smooth
   d. lance is to sharp

Relationship: _____

_____

_____

_____

Challenge: Make up your own

Write a comparison using the words in the box below. (Hint: There are three possible analogies.) Then write the relationship on the lines provided.

toxic	computer	safe	shrink
chair	magnify	camera	car
vehicle	lens	screen	furniture

Analogy: _____ is to _____ as _____ is to _____.

Relationship: _____

_____

Word Families

*The words in **boldface** in the sentences below are related to words introduced in Units 9–12. For example, the nouns* enclosure *and* procedure *in item 1 are related to the verbs* proceed *(Unit 10) and* enclose *(Unit 9). Based on your understanding of the unit words that follow, circle the related word in **boldface** that best completes each sentence.*

circular	discipline	distress	drench	dwell
elevate	enclose	extreme	earnest	heroic
inspire	magnify	nourish	proceed	reflect
register	tardy	toxic	uneasy	variety

1. The zoo recently built an air-conditioned (**enclosure/procedure**) for its polar bears.

2. It is the principal's job to take (**varietal/disciplinary**) action when students are unruly.

3. A homeless family's greatest need is a (**dwelling/magnification**).

4. The President presented the pilots with medals for their (**uneasiness/heroism**) during the rescue mission.

5. It was so cold that we had no feeling in our (**extremities/tardiness**).

6. The (**gradualness/pointlessness**) of the speaker's jokes annoyed the audience.

7. (**Registration/Elevation**) forms for summer camp must be completed by the end of March.

8. The veterinarian said that the stray cat we found needed lots of (**earnestness/nourishment**).

9. The Nobel Prize winner's (**inspirational/distressing**) speech restored our hope for the future.

10. The safest toys for young children are made of (**nontoxic/semicircular**) materials.

Word Games

Use the clues below to complete the crossword puzzle.
(All of the answers are words from Units 9–12.)

Across
1. to concentrate
3. to clutch or seize
5. an underground prison
11.
12. late
13. to throw back
14. annoying

Down
2. a splurge or binge
4. to tremble
6. a muttered complaint
7. a lack of sameness
8. to make unhappy
9. to put through a strainer
10. a settlement or pact

Definitions

Study the spelling, pronunciation, part of speech, and definition given for each of the words below. Write the word in the blank space in the sentence that follows. Then read the synonyms and antonyms.

1. **abstract**
   (ab 'strakt)

   (adj.) having to do with an idea or quality rather than an object; hard to understand; (in art) with little likeness to real people or things
   A character in a book may stand for an _____ idea such as kindness.

   SYNONYMS: conceptual, theoretical; obscure; a summary
   ANTONYMS: actual, physical, real, concrete; realistic

2. **ally**
   (v., ə 'lī;
   n., 'a lī)

   (v.) to unite or join for a special purpose
   Parents may _____ themselves with teachers to tutor students who need extra help.

   (n.) a person or country joined with another for a special purpose
   Great Britain was an _____ of the United States in World War II.

   SYNONYMS: to unite, associate, combine; a partner, associate
   ANTONYMS: an enemy, opponent

3. **appoint**
   (ə 'point)

   (v.) to choose (someone) for a position or duty; to decide on
   It is the responsibility of the mayor to _____ a police chief.

   SYNONYMS: to designate, assign, elect
   ANTONYMS: to dismiss, remove, suspend

4. **attentive**
   (ə 'ten tiv)

   (adj.) paying attention; thoughtful and polite
   When you write a composition, you should be _____ to spelling and punctuation.

   SYNONYMS: observant, alert; considerate, courteous
   ANTONYMS: inattentive, unobservant; inconsiderate

5. **bonus**
   ('bō nəs)

   (n.) something extra or beyond what is owed or expected
   Many companies give their employees a _____ at the end of the year.

   SYNONYMS: an addition, reward, benefit, gift, prize
   ANTONYMS: a penalty, deduction, fine

6. **carefree**
   ('kâr frē)

   (adj.) without troubles, worries, or responsibilities
   Summer vacation is usually a _____ time.

   SYNONYMS: untroubled, lighthearted
   ANTONYMS: troubled, worried, anxious

Assembly lines are still used in the **manufacture** (word 8) of automobiles but many jobs once performed by people are now done by robotic machines.

7. **courtesy**
('kər tə sē)

(n.) polite, thoughtful, or considerate behavior; a polite act; a favor
Customers appreciate being treated with _____.

SYNONYMS: care, concern, regard, politeness, thoughtfulness
ANTONYMS: discourtesy, disregard, rudeness

8. **manufacture**
(man yə 'fak chər)

(v.) to make something, especially using machinery; to make up
I had to _____ an excuse.

(n.) the making of something, especially using machinery
A factory in our town specializes in the _____ of furniture.

SYNONYMS: to assemble, construct, build, produce; to invent, concoct

9. **mistrust**
(mis 'trəst)

(n.) a lack of confidence
Some people have a deep _____ of politicians.

(v.) to have no confidence in; to be suspicious of; to doubt
Sometimes I _____ my own judgment.

SYNONYMS: doubt, uncertainty, suspicion; to question, disbelieve
ANTONYMS: trust, confidence, belief; to trust, believe

10. **noticeable**
('nō tə sə bəl)

(adj.) easy to see; likely to be observed; worthy of attention
We saw a _____ improvement in their play.

SYNONYMS: observable, visible, obvious, evident
ANTONYMS: overlooked, hidden, obscure

11. **overthrow**
(ō vər 'thrō)

(v.) to overturn; to bring about the fall or end of
The rebels will _____ the cruel ruler.

(n.) an act of bringing down; defeat
The people celebrated the _____ of the heartless king.

SYNONYMS: to remove, bring down, topple, destroy, ruin, upset; collapse, ruin
ANTONYMS: to preserve, support, restore

12. **peculiar**
(pi 'kyül yər)

(adj.) not like the normal or usual; odd or curious; belonging to a particular group, person, place, or thing
Everyone is talking about the _____ weather this year.

SYNONYMS: special, particular, bizarre, unusual, strange, distinctive, unique
ANTONYMS: ordinary, routine, regular, normal, common

Match the Meaning

For each item below choose the word whose meaning is suggested by the clue given. Then write the word in the space provided.

1. Our advisor can _____ a leader for our debating team.
   a. overthrow   b. manufacture   c. abstract   d. appoint

2. To bring about the end of something is to _____ it.
   a. mistrust   b. overthrow   c. appoint   d. manufacture

3. If you do not have confidence in something, you _____ it.
   a. appoint   b. ally   c. mistrust   d. manufacture

4. Something that is unusual or odd is _____.
   a. attentive   b. abstract   c. carefree   d. peculiar

5. If something is easy to see, it is _____.
   a. noticeable   b. abstract   c. attentive   d. carefree

6. When you get a free gift with a subscription, you get a(n) _____.
   a. abstract   b. bonus   c. ally   d. manufacture

7. Speakers appreciate audiences that are _____.
   a. attentive   b. abstract   c. carefree   d. peculiar

8. To be kind or polite to other people is to behave with _____.
   a. mistrust   b. manufacture   c. courtesy   d. bonus

9. A person who feels _____ does not worry.
   a. noticeable   b. carefree   c. peculiar   d. attentive

10. The workers in a factory _____ products.
    a. manufacture   b. abstract   c. mistrust   d. appoint

11. Something that is about ideas and qualities rather than people is _____.
    a. attentive   b. carefree   c. abstract   d. noticeable

12. You may _____ yourself with others to improve your community.
    a. ally   b. overthrow   c. appoint   d. mistrust

Synonyms

*For each item below choose the word that is most nearly the **same** in meaning as the word or phrase in **boldface**. Then write your choice on the line provided.*

1. **doubted** the evidence
   a. mistrusted b. overthrew c. appointed d. manufactured _____

2. received an unexpected **reward**
   a. overthrow b. ally c. manufacture d. bonus _____

3. **produce** lawn mowers
   a. manufacture b. abstract c. mistrust d. appoint _____

4. **topple** a government
   a. appoint b. overthrow c. mistrust d. manufacture _____

5. faithful **supporters**
   a. abstracts b. allies c. bonuses d. courtesies _____

6. walked with a **distinct** limp
   a. attentive b. carefree c. noticeable d. peculiar _____

Antonyms

*For each item below choose the word that is most nearly **opposite** in meaning to the word or phrase in **boldface**. Then write your choice on the line provided.*

1. **anxious** tourists
   a. attentive b. carefree c. noticeable d. peculiar _____

2. **neglectful** waiters
   a. abstract b. peculiar c. carefree d. attentive _____

3. frightened by **ordinary** noises
   a. attentive b. abstract c. peculiar d. noticeable _____

4. **realistic** paintings
   a. abstract b. noticeable c. carefree d. attentive _____

5. show **rudeness** to others
   a. overthrow b. mistrust c. bonus d. courtesy _____

6. **dismiss** the commander
   a. overthrow b. appoint c. ally d. manufacture _____

Completing the Sentence

From the list of words on pages 106–107, choose the one that best completes each item below. Write the word in the space provided. (You may have to change the word's ending.)

PAYING ATTENTION

■ A guest speaker visited our science class last week. We were on our best behavior and tried to be _____ during the talk.

■ The speaker discussed many _____ ideas about time and space that were very hard to understand.

■ To make things more difficult, the speaker's voice had a(n) _____ singsong tone that was distracting.

■ We applauded our guest politely, but some students gave a(n) _____ sigh of relief when the speech ended.

NOW THAT'S JUSTICE!

■ In 1967, President Lyndon Johnson _____ Thurgood Marshall to be the first African American to serve on the Supreme Court.

■ For many years Marshall had been a lawyer for the National Association for the Advancement of Colored People (NAACP). During those years he had argued more than thirty cases before the Supreme Court. Many of these cases helped to _____ laws that had discriminated against African Americans.

■ At first some people _____ Marshall and opposed his nomination.

■ But Marshall's _____ supported him, and he took his place on the Court. He went on to become one of America's greatest justices.

THE BUSINESS OF PLAY

■ A lot of people think it must be fun to work in a toy factory. They would probably be surprised to learn that the _____ of toys is not a game.

■ You may think of toys in connection with _____ play, but to toy companies they are serious business.

■ In some factories bosses offer cash _____ to workers who suggest ways to speed up production.

■ Owners of toy stores often get samples of new toys as a _____.
In return for the favor, the owners may test the toys with their customers and then tell the companies how well the toys are liked.

1. Which is **abstract**?
   a. water
   b. food
   c. thought
   d. metal

2. I might **mistrust** a TV ad that
   a. does not give me any facts
   b. is on after midnight
   c. uses actors and costumes
   d. raises honest questions

3. The President may **appoint**
   a. starting pitchers
   b. your town's mayor
   c. talk show hosts
   d. cabinet members

4. A **noticeable** difference may be
   a. hard to see
   b. hard to describe
   c. confusing to someone
   d. obvious to everyone

5. Which might **carefree** people do?
   a. worry about everything
   b. argue with their friends
   c. whistle their favorite tunes
   d. work on their homework

6. A **peculiar** outfit is one that is
   a. expensive
   b. strange
   c. ragged
   d. colorful

7. Which may be **overthrown**?
   a. kings and queens
   b. salt and pepper
   c. shoes and socks
   d. dogs and cats

8. Someone who is your **ally** will
   a. gossip about you
   b. be on your side
   c. borrow your books
   d. ignore you

9. I get a **bonus** from my book club
   a. if I order lots of books
   b. if I ask nicely for one
   c. if I break my leg
   d. if I owe it lots of money

10. If you **manufacture** excuses, you
    a. open a factory
    b. buy them at a discount
    c. think them up yourself
    d. tell the truth

11. Which comment shows **courtesy**?
    a. "Who asked you?"
    b. "That's not a good plan."
    c. "Get out of my way!"
    d. "May I serve you more soup?"

12. You'll be more **attentive** if you
    a. listen or look closely
    b. take attendance
    c. install a smoke alarm
    d. curl up on the couch

Definitions

Study the spelling, pronunciation, part of speech, and definition given for each of the words below. Write the word in the blank space in the sentence that follows. Then read the synonyms and antonyms.

1. **absolute**
   ('ab sə lüt)

   (adj.) without flaws or imperfections; without limits; without doubt
   The witness swore to tell the _____ truth.

   SYNONYMS: pure, perfect; entire, whole, complete, unlimited; certain, sure
   ANTONYMS: flawed; limited, incomplete, restricted; uncertain

2. **arena**
   (ə 'rē nə)

   (n.) an enclosed space used for sports or shows; a field of interest, activity, conflict, or debate
   The senator has been in the political _____ ever since she was elected president of her high school class.

   SYNONYMS: a stadium, theater, auditorium; field, scene

3. **compliment**
   ('käm plə mənt)

   (n.) a remark or action that shows admiration, praise, or approval; (used in the plural) good wishes
   Everyone likes to receive a _____.
   (v.) to give praise or admiration to
   The losing team _____ the winners on their victory.

   SYNONYMS: congratulations; regards; to flatter, applaud, salute
   ANTONYMS: blame, criticism; to insult, denounce, criticize

4. **deliberate**
   (v., di 'li bə rāt;
   adj., di 'li bə rət)

   (v.) to think about or discuss very carefully
   A jury may _____ for days before reaching a verdict.
   (adj.) done or said on purpose; careful; at a slow pace
   A person may tell a _____ lie to avoid blame.

   SYNONYMS: to consider, debate, weigh; intentional; careful, thoughtful, purposeful
   ANTONYMS: unwitting, impulsive; careless, haphazard, hasty, hurried

5. **dense**
   (dens)

   (adj.) close or packed together; thick; stupid
   A _____ crowd blocked the entrance to the building.

   SYNONYMS: compact, solid, crowded; dull-witted, thickheaded
   ANTONYMS: sparse, open, scattered, thin; alert, clever, smart

6. **dominant**
   ('dä mə nənt)

   (adj.) above all others; leading or controlling; having the most power
   The President is usually the _____ figure in his or her political party.

   SYNONYMS: chief, main, first, foremost; commanding, controlling
   ANTONYMS: inferior, secondary; humble, modest

Hazardous (word 7) waste can cause serious damage to the environment and health problems for people exposed to it.

7. **hazardous**
('ha zər dəs)

(adj.) involving risk or danger
Special containers are used for disposing of _____ waste.

SYNONYMS: dangerous, perilous, risky, unsafe
ANTONYMS: safe, certain, secure

8. **huddle**
('hə dəl)

(v.) to crowd close together; to form a closely packed group; to get together to discuss something
Campers may _____ around a fire on a cold night.

(n.) a tightly packed group; a meeting or discussion; in football, a quick meeting of players on the field to plan the next play
The coaches held a brief _____ on the sidelines.

SYNONYMS: to bunch, cluster, crowd; to gather; a bunch, conference

9. **necessity**
(ni 'se sə tē)

(n.) something that cannot be avoided or done without; great need
Water is a _____ for life.

SYNONYMS: a requirement, essential, must; want
ANTONYMS: an option, extra, luxury

10. **offend**
(ə 'fend)

(v.) to break a law or rule; to cause hurt feelings, anger, or injury
Thoughtless behavior will _____ most people.

SYNONYMS: to embarrass, displease, insult, upset, irritate, annoy, wound
ANTONYMS: to please, charm, soothe

11. **regain**
(rē 'gān)

(v.) to get back; to reach again
It takes time to _____ your strength after an illness.

SYNONYM: to recover
ANTONYMS: to lose, forfeit

12. **thorough**
('thər ō)

(adj.) carried out to completion; complete in every detail; extremely careful or exact
The dentist gave me a _____ checkup.

SYNONYMS: exhaustive, extensive, total, full
ANTONYMS: incomplete, partial, limited, unfinished; cursory, inadequate

For each item below choose the word whose meaning is suggested by the clue given. Then write the word in the space provided.

1. To think carefully about something is to _____.
   a. offend   b. compliment   c. regain   d. deliberate

2. When people say things that hurt your feelings, they _____ you.
   a. huddle   b. offend   c. deliberate   d. compliment

3. A group of people crowded close together is a(n) _____.
   a. necessity   b. arena   c. huddle   d. compliment

4. For spring cleaning to be _____, it should be done room by room.
   a. dense   b. dominant   c. absolute   d. thorough

5. Skating on thin ice is _____.
   a. hazardous   b. thorough   c. deliberate   d. dominant

6. A(n) _____ is an indoor space used for sports or shows.
   a. huddle   b. arena   c. necessity   d. compliment

7. When you get back something you have lost, you _____ it.
   a. compliment   b. deliberate   c. regain   d. offend

8. A fog that you cannot see through may be described as _____.
   a. dense   b. absolute   c. dominant   d. thorough

9. Power that has no limits is _____ power.
   a. deliberate   b. dense   c. absolute   d. hazardous

10. The member of a group who has the most influence and control is the
    _____ individual.
    a. absolute   b. dominant   c. thorough   d. dense

11. When someone pays me a(n) _____, I feel proud and happy.
    a. compliment   b. arena   c. huddle   d. necessity

12. A(n) _____ is something that you cannot do without.
    a. huddle   b. compliment   c. arena   d. necessity

Synonyms

*For each item below choose the word that is most nearly the **same** in meaning as the word or phrase in **boldface**. Then write your choice on the line provided.*

1. **crowd** under the umbrella
   a. huddle   b. regain   c. deliberate   d. compliment   _____

2. attended a game at the county **auditorium**
   a. huddle   b. necessity   c. compliment   d. arena   _____

3. **congratulate** the winner of the scholarship
   a. compliment   b. offend   c. regain   d. deliberate   _____

4. **displeased** the audience
   a. deliberated   b. offended   c. regained   d. complimented   _____

5. one of the **requirements** for the job
   a. arenas   b. necessities   c. huddles   d. compliments   _____

6. a **dangerous** path
   a. dense   b. dominant   c. hazardous   d. thorough   _____

Antonyms

*For each item below choose the word that is most nearly **opposite** in meaning to the word or phrase in **boldface**. Then write your choice on the line provided.*

1. a **secondary** share of the market
   a. dense   b. hazardous   c. dominant   d. thorough   _____

2. flew through **thin** clouds
   a. absolute   b. dense   c. deliberate   d. hazardous   _____

3. did an **incomplete** job
   a. dense   b. hazardous   c. thorough   d. dominant   _____

4. **lose** control of the vehicle
   a. compliment   b. deliberate   c. offend   d. regain   _____

5. have **limited** control
   a. absolute   b. dense   c. hazardous   d. deliberate   _____

6. at a **hurried** pace
   a. dense   b. absolute   c. deliberate   d. dominant   _____

Completing the Sentence

From the list of words on pages 112–113, choose the one that best completes each item below. Write the word in the space provided. (You may have to change the word's ending.)

UP, UP, AND AWAY

■ Flying a hot-air balloon is an exciting experience. But if you do not use good sense and follow proper safety precautions, it can also be _____.

■ Clear, calm weather and open airspace are _____ for safe balloon travel.

■ Darkness, bad weather, or _____ fog can hide dangers, such as trees, wires, and buildings.

CHESS, ANYONE?

■ In the _____ of strategy games, chess has many devoted fans. Chess is one of the most ancient games in the field, dating back to at least the sixth century.

■ Once chess was a favored game of the royal and the rich. Today, however, it is enjoyed by people from all walks of life. When skilled players compete at outdoor tables in city parks, spectators _____ around to watch them.

■ The game's _____ players stun their opponents with unexpected moves. Some of these top players have even tried their skills against those of a computer.

■ Players use clocks to limit the time they may _____ between moves.

■ A chess game may end with a narrow win or a draw. But some matches finish with one player achieving a(n) _____, flawless victory.

APOLOGY ACCEPTED

■ The other day I made a serious mistake. Without thinking, I made an unkind remark that _____ my best friend.

■ When I saw the hurt look on her face, I felt ashamed of myself. All I wanted was to _____ her trust.

■ I offered a sincere and _____ apology. I also promised her that I would be more considerate of her feelings from now on.

■ My friend _____ me for admitting my mistake and then forgave me. I am so glad we are best friends again!

*Circle the letter next to the word or expression that best completes the sentence or answers the question. Pay special attention to the word in **boldface.***

1. If you **regain** the lead, you get
   a. a flashlight
   b. the daily paper
   c. a free movie ticket
   d. back in first place

2. Why might a group of people form a **huddle**?
   a. to drink hot cocoa
   b. to do laundry
   c. to talk things over
   d. to catch a fish

3. Toys **hazardous** to a baby might
   a. have floppy ears
   b. have sharp edges
   c. have cute faces
   d. have orange fur

4. When I go at a **deliberate** speed,
   a. I walk slowly
   b. I think too much
   c. I ride in a taxi cab
   d. I deserve a speeding ticket

5. A **dominant** person
   a. sings and dances
   b. eats and drinks
   c. leads and controls
   d. laughs and cries

6. A **thorough** report should include
   a. every detail
   b. spelling mistakes
   c. graphs and charts
   d. an E-mail address

7. Which is a true **necessity**?
   a. talking on the telephone
   b. sleeping ten hours a night
   c. showering every day
   d. having food and shelter

8. I might **offend** you if I asked
   a. "How about some milk?"
   b. "How silly can you be?"
   c. "Shall we sit together?"
   d. "What time is it?"

9. We might go to an **arena** to see
   a. a menu
   b. an encyclopedia
   c. a dentist
   d. a hockey game

10. With **absolute** proof, there is no
    a. evidence
    b. music
    c. doubt
    d. hot water

11. If I want to pay you a **compliment**, I might say
    a. "Nice outfit!"
    b. "That's a terrible plan!"
    c. "Good grief!"
    d. "Not on your life!"

12. A forest that is **dense** is
    a. green
    b. thick
    c. nearby
    d. far away

Definitions

Study the spelling, pronunciation, part of speech, and definition given for each of the words below. Write the word in the blank space in the sentence that follows. Then read the synonyms and antonyms.

1. **adopt**
   (ə 'däpt)

   (v.) to take another person's child into one's family; to use as one's own; to accept or approve
   A family may _____ an orphan from a war-torn country.

   SYNONYMS: to choose, select; to endorse, approve, assume
   ANTONYMS: to reject, disown, refuse, renounce, abandon, desert

2. **agile**
   ('a jəl)

   (adj.) capable of moving easily, quickly, and gracefully; mentally quick
   Squirrels are _____ climbers.

   SYNONYMS: nimble, spry, limber; alert, sharp
   ANTONYMS: clumsy, heavy; slow

3. **analyze**
   ('a nəl īz)

   (v.) to study the parts of something in order to understand what it is, how it is put together, or how it works; to study carefully or in detail
   Scientists _____ moon rocks to learn more about what the moon is made of.

   SYNONYMS: to examine, inspect, investigate, evaluate, test; to dissect

4. **assist**
   (ə 'sist)

   (v.) to give help or support
   Several doctors may _____ a surgeon during an operation.

   (n.) the act of helping; in sports, an action that helps a teammate score or get a player out
   A hockey player may receive credit for an _____.

   SYNONYMS: to help, aid, boost, contribute
   ANTONYMS: to hamper, hinder, obstruct; an obstruction

5. **babble**
   ('ba bəl)

   (v.) to talk foolishly or too much; to make meaningless sounds; to make a gurgling sound
   Some people can _____ on the telephone for hours.

   (n.) a mix of meaningless sounds, usually as made by water
   The soft _____ of a creek can be very relaxing.

   SYNONYMS: to chatter, jabber, prattle, gab; drivel, nonsense, murmur

6. **captivity**
   (kap 'ti və tē)

   (n.) the state of being confined or held against one's will
   Some prisoners of war have been held in _____ for years.

   SYNONYMS: slavery, confinement, custody, restraint, imprisonment, bondage
   ANTONYMS: freedom, liberty, independence

To be a successful rock climber
it helps to be strong and **agile**
(word 2).

7. **drab**
(drab)

(n.) an olive brown or brownish gray color
The old canvas tents were a faded _____.

(adj.) marked by dullness; like the color drab; cheerless
A good book is good company on a _____ *and
rainy afternoon.*

SYNONYMS: brownish; dull, dingy, colorless, uninteresting, lackluster; dreary
ANTONYMS: colorful, cheerful, bright

8. **fatal**
('fā təl)

(adj.) causing death, destruction, or ruin
One passenger suffered a _____ *injury.*

SYNONYMS: deadly, lethal, disastrous; decisive, fateful
ANTONYMS: harmless, healthful

9. **generosity**
(je nə 'rä sə tē)

(n.) the quality of being charitable to others in thought or action;
willingness to give; an act of giving
The heiress is well known for her _____.

SYNONYMS: charity, unselfishness
ANTONYMS: stinginess, cheapness, greed

10. **genuine**
('jen yə wən)

(adj.) real, actually being what something appears to be; true or
reliable; sincere or honest
I found a _____ *fossil in my yard.*

SYNONYMS: authentic, original, actual; valid; trustworthy, earnest, frank
ANTONYMS: fake, false, artificial, unreal; insincere, phony, pretended

11. **illegal**
(i 'lē gəl)

(adj.) against the law; against the rules
Stealing is an _____ *act.*

SYNONYMS: unlawful, criminal, outlawed; forbidden, prohibited
ANTONYMS: legal, lawful, allowed

12. **merit**
('mer ət)

(n.) the fact of deserving something; a quality that deserves reward or
praise; worth or value
Her science project has great _____.

(v.) to deserve, be worthy of
His poems _____ *being published.*

SYNONYMS: excellence, virtue, quality, worthiness; to earn, justify, rate
ANTONYMS: disgrace, dishonor, failing, shortcoming, defect, flaw, fault

For each item below choose the word whose meaning is suggested by the clue given. Then write the word in the space provided.

1. If your work has _____, it deserves praise or reward.
   a. generosity   b. babble   c. captivity   d. merit

2. To _____ a pet is to care for it as part of one's family.
   a. analyze   b. adopt   c. merit   d. assist

3. When I talk foolishly or too much, I _____.
   a. adopt   b. assist   c. babble   d. analyze

4. Fabric that is _____ is neither colorful nor cheery.
   a. illegal   b. genuine   c. agile   d. drab

5. Something that causes death is _____.
   a. fatal   b. drab   c. illegal   d. genuine

6. People in _____ are held against their will.
   a. babble   b. captivity   c. drab   d. generosity

7. A(n) _____ action is against the law or the rules.
   a. illegal   b. agile   c. genuine   d. fatal

8. Someone who has a(n) _____ mind is quick and sharp.
   a. drab   b. illegal   c. agile   d. genuine

9. If something is _____, it is truly what it appears to be.
   a. fatal   b. genuine   c. drab   d. agile

10. When you help someone, you _____ that person.
    a. assist   b. adopt   c. babble   d. analyze

11. When I study how something is put together, I _____ it.
    a. assist   b. merit   c. analyze   d. adopt

12. _____ is a willingness to give to others.
    a. Babble   b. Merit   c. Captivity   d. Generosity

Synonyms

*For each item below choose the word that is most nearly the **same** in meaning as the word or phrase in **boldface**. Then write your choice on the line provided.*

1. **examine** our mistakes
   a. merit   b. analyze   c. babble   d. assist   _____

2. **chatters** about nothing
   a. babbles   b. assists   c. merits   d. adopts   _____

3. suffered in **bondage**
   a. merit   b. generosity   c. babble   d. captivity   _____

4. an idea of little or no **value**
   a. assist   b. babble   c. merit   d. generosity   _____

5. an **authentic** Civil War sword
   a. genuine   b. illegal   c. drab   d. agile   _____

6. a **deadly** poison
   a. illegal   b. genuine   c. fatal   d. drab   _____

Antonyms

*For each item below choose the word that is most nearly **opposite** in meaning to the word or phrase in **boldface**. Then write your choice on the line provided.*

1. **hindered** the investigation
   a. assisted   b. adopted   c. merited   d. analyzed   _____

2. **abandoned** the puppy
   a. analyzed   b. assisted   c. adopted   d. merited   _____

3. a **lawful** act
   a. agile   b. illegal   c. genuine   d. drab   _____

4. wore **colorful** costumes
   a. illegal   b. fatal   c. drab   d. genuine   _____

5. famous for their **cheapness**
   a. generosity   b. captivity   c. merit   d. babble   _____

6. **clumsy** mountain goats
   a. fatal   b. illegal   c. drab   d. agile   _____

Completing the Sentence

From the list of words on pages 118–119, choose the one that best completes each item below. Write the word in the space provided. (You may have to change the word's ending.)

A YEARLY EVENT

■ Each year our town holds a fall festival. It is lively and noisy and fun for everyone. But the _____ of the crowd quiets down when it comes time for the mayor's ceremony.

■ The highlight of this ceremony is the announcement of the two people who _____ the Best Neighbor Award.

■ This award is given to people for outstanding _____ to fellow citizens who are in need.

■ You can see the _____ delight on the winners' faces when the mayor hands them big silver keys to the city.

CLUES TO POLLUTION

■ You may think that the mud on a riverbank looks _____ and ordinary. But scientists know that even though it looks dull, it may contain clues to pollution.

■ Scientists can _____ the mud to find out if any harmful chemicals are present in the soil and water.

■ This is one way that scientists can tell if there has been _____ dumping of waste materials.

■ The data scientists gather from the mud can _____ them in finding and stopping the polluters.

DON'T TRY THIS AT HOME

■ Baby animals are cute. A bear cub may look so cuddly that you might think it would be fun to _____ one.

■ It is important to remember that a wild animal can be dangerous. To try to raise one in your home could be a(n) _____ mistake.

■ As the playful cub grows more _____ and strong, it soon becomes too big and dangerous to be a family pet.

■ Then you would have to find a home for the animal in a zoo. You couldn't just set the bear free in a forest. A wild animal raised in _____ may not have the skills it would need to survive in the wild.

Word Associations

*Circle the letter next to the word or expression that best completes the sentence or answers the question. Pay special attention to the word in **boldface**.*

1. I **babble** when I get too
   a. excited
   b. bored
   c. angry
   d. serious

2. A **drab** outfit would be
   a. colorless or dull
   b. too small or too big
   c. made of scratchy cloth
   d. out of fashion

3. It is **illegal** to use
   a. pay telephones
   b. fake money
   c. common sense
   d. pencils

4. You would **merit** a raise if your boss
   a. owned the business
   b. knew your name
   c. thought you did poor work
   d. thought you did great work

5. A person who is **genuine** is
   a. cheerful
   b. nervous
   c. sincere
   d. clumsy

6. You can show **generosity** by
   a. opening a bank account
   b. exercising every day
   c. doing your homework
   d. sharing your lunch

7. Which might be **fatal** if eaten?
   a. applesauce
   b. drain cleaner
   c. stale crackers
   d. hot peppers

8. The state **adopts** a law if the
   a. children need parents
   b. governor takes in a family
   c. lawmakers approve it
   d. lawmakers reject it

9. You would find animals in **captivity**
   a. in the wild
   b. up a tree
   c. free to come and go
   d. in a zoo

10. When I want to **assist** someone, I will ask
    a. "May I be of help?"
    b. "Can't you do it yourself?"
    c. "What time is it?"
    d. "Do I have to?"

11. Having an **agile** mind helps you
    a. to do cartwheels
    b. to take a nap
    c. to feed your pet
    d. to catch on quickly

12. If you **analyze** a song, you'll find
    a. dots and dashes
    b. bells and whistles
    c. rhythms and melodies
    d. bones and muscles

Definitions

Study the spelling, pronunciation, part of speech, and definition given for each of the words below. Write the word in the blank space in the sentence that follows. Then read the synonyms and antonyms.

1. **adorn**
   (ə ˈdôrn)

   (v.) to add to the appearance of, especially with pretty objects; to dress up
      Fresh flowers and beautiful linens _____ the dining room table.

   SYNONYMS: to decorate, ornament, enrich, grace, beautify, enhance
   ANTONYMS: to damage, mar, blemish

2. **appropriate**
   (v., ə ˈprō prē āt;
   adj., ə ˈprō prē ət)

   (v.) to take over or use as one's own, often without permission; to set apart for a certain purpose
      A brother or sister may _____ your favorite book.
   (adj.) suitable or fitting
      It is _____ to wear a warm hat in the winter.

   SYNONYMS: to seize, confiscate, steal; to allot; correct, suitable, proper
   ANTONYMS: unfitting, unsuitable, inappropriate, improper

3. **assemble**
   (ə ˈsem bəl)

   (v.) to meet or bring together; to put or fit parts together
      On Thanksgiving family members _____ to enjoy a holiday feast.

   SYNONYMS: to convene, gather, congregate; to build, construct, join, connect
   ANTONYMS: to scatter, break up, disperse; to separate, divide

4. **colossal**
   (kə ˈlä səl)

   (adj.) amazingly large, great, or powerful in size or degree
      Whale watchers hope for a glimpse of a _____ blue whale.

   SYNONYMS: enormous, huge, gigantic, massive, immense
   ANTONYMS: tiny, small, little

5. **effective**
   (i ˈfek tiv)

   (adj.) producing a desired or conclusive result; having a strong impact; starting as of a particular date or time
      The team that makes the most _____ presentation will win the debate.

   SYNONYMS: capable, potent, impressive, striking, compelling; starting, beginning
   ANTONYMS: ineffective, futile, useless, weak

6. **frail**
   (frāl)

   (adj.) weak or lacking strength; likely to give in to temptation
      Our class project is to send cheerful greeting cards to children who are in _____ health.

   SYNONYMS: delicate, feeble, sickly, slight, fragile, flimsy, brittle, breakable
   ANTONYMS: sturdy, robust, hardy, healthy; firm, strong, solid

This **colossal** (word 4) pyramid was built about a thousand years ago in what is now southern Mexico. It stands upon the site of an even older Mayan city known as Chichén Itzá.

7. **hostage**
   ('häs tij)

(n.) a person held prisoner by another or by an enemy, and used in bargaining for certain demands
   The hijacker took one _____.
SYNONYMS: a prisoner, pawn

8. **landslide**
   ('land slīd)

(n.) a fast downhill movement of rocks or soil; any mass that slides down; a lopsided victory in an election
   A week of heavy rain caused a _____.
SYNONYMS: an avalanche; a rout

9. **rampage**
   ('ram pāj)

(v.) to rush around wildly or violently
   A herd of frightened animals may _____.
(n.) violent, reckless, or wild behavior
   The news carried a story about looters on a _____.
SYNONYMS: to rage; a riot, uproar, turmoil, frenzy

10. **scamper**
    ('skam pər)

(v.) to run or move quickly or playfully
   Children usually _____ *around a playground.*
SYNONYMS: to dash, scurry, hurry, scoot, romp
ANTONYMS: to lumber, lag, dawdle, stroll

11. **symptom**
    ('sim təm)

(n.) a sign of illness or of a physical problem; a sign that something else exists or is happening
   Fever is one _____ *of the flu.*
SYNONYMS: a signal, clue, indication; evidence

12. **warrant**
    ('wôr ənt)

(n.) a written order that allows for legal action
   The police got a _____ *to search the suspect's garage.*
(v.) to declare for certain; to approve or guarantee; to serve as reason for
   A deep cut may _____ *stitches.*
SYNONYMS: an authorization, guarantee, assurance, permit; to pledge, certify, promise, entitle, authorize, justify

Match the Meaning

For each item below choose the word whose meaning is suggested by the clue given. Then write the word in the space provided.

1. To run happily across a field is to _____.
   a. appropriate   b. rampage   c. assemble   d. scamper

2. When you trim a hat with ribbons, you _____ it.
   a. appropriate   b. adorn   c. warrant   d. assemble

3. To use something without permission is to _____ it.
   a. rampage   b. warrant   c. appropriate   d. assemble

4. If you have a fever and a rash, you have _____ of measles.
   a. warrants   b. landslides   c. hostages   d. symptoms

5. The date when something begins is its _____ date.
   a. effective   b. colossal   c. appropriate   d. frail

6. Kidnappers take _____ to get money.
   a. warrants   b. hostages   c. landslides   d. symptoms

7. An order that permits the arrest of someone is a _____.
   a. warrant   b. rampage   c. landslide   d. symptom

8. The _____ skeleton belonged to a gigantic dinosaur.
   a. frail   b. appropriate   c. colossal   d. effective

9. Something that is easily broken is _____.
   a. effective   b. frail   c. appropriate   d. colossal

10. The reckless actions of a mob may be described as a _____.
    a. rampage   b. hostage   c. landslide   d. scamper

11. When you put a model airplane together, you _____ it.
    a. warrant   b. appropriate   c. assemble   d. adorn

12. The rocks and mud that block a road are the result of a _____.
    a. warrant   b. symptom   c. hostage   d. landslide

Synonyms

*For each item below choose the word that is most nearly the **same** in meaning as the word or phrase in **boldface**. Then write your choice on the line provided.*

1. **signs** of trouble
   a. warrants   b. hostages   c. landslides   d. symptoms   _____

2. a **pledge** to finish the job
   a. hostage   b. rampage   c. warrant   d. symptom   _____

3. communicate with the **prisoner**
   a. rampage   b. landslide   c. symptom   d. hostage   _____

4. **rioted** in the streets
   a. rampaged   b. assembled   c. appropriated   d. scampered   _____

5. **ornamented** with jewels
   a. scampered   b. adorned   c. assembled   d. rampaged   _____

6. buried by an **avalanche**
   a. hostage   b. landslide   c. symptom   d. warrant   _____

Antonyms

*For each item below choose the word that is most nearly **opposite** in meaning to the word or phrase in **boldface**. Then write your choice on the line provided.*

1. a **robust** person
   a. appropriate   b. frail   c. effective   d. colossal   _____

2. made a **little** mistake
   a. effective   b. appropriate   c. frail   d. colossal   _____

3. **dawdled** on the lawn
   a. scampered   b. warranted   c. adorned   d. assembled   _____

4. **unsuitable** clothing for a camping trip
   a. frail   b. effective   c. colossal   d. appropriate   _____

5. a **useless** medicine
   a. frail   b. effective   c. colossal   d. appropriate   _____

6. where the group will **scatter**
   a. rampage   b. scamper   c. appropriate   d. assemble   _____

Completing the Sentence

From the list of words on pages 124–125, choose the one that best completes each item below. Write the word in the space provided. (You may have to change the word's ending.)

A GLORIOUS FOURTH

■ On the Fourth of July, the people who live in our town _____ peacefully in the park for a picnic and fireworks.

■ Everyone, young and old, comes to the party. Seniors from the high school volunteer to bring people who are too _____ to get to the park on their own.

■ Members of the picnic committee _____ the trees and the bandstand with red, white, and blue balloons.

■ The band plays patriotic songs and old favorites. People eat and talk, and young children _____ on the lawns, playing tag and hide-and-seek. Everyone has a wonderful time.

IN HARM'S WAY

■ In wartime invading armies _____ through cities and towns, destroying everything that lies in their path.

■ The troops _____ any food and supplies they want. They may even take over people's homes.

■ A village or an entire region can be held _____ by the invaders.

■ Such actions _____ a military response from the defending armies. The victims of the conflict also need aid from international relief agencies.

HOMES AT RISK

■ All along the beautiful coast of California, people build homes on the hills that overlook the ocean. But the _____ forces of nature can bring danger to those who live on the hillsides.

■ A long period of dry weather is one _____ that trouble may lie ahead. Dry trees and grasses can easily catch fire. Every year some houses are badly damaged or burn to the ground.

■ When heavy rains come, the homeowners worry about _____.

■ Even concrete and stone do not always give _____ protection from the power of nature.

*Circle the letter next to the word or expression that best completes the sentence or answers the question. Pay special attention to the word in **boldface**.*

1. **Effective** exercise helps you
   a. learn to cook
   b. speak Latin
   c. finish your homework
   d. get in shape

2. To **assemble** a jigsaw puzzle, you
   a. lose the pieces
   b. count the pieces
   c. put the pieces back in the box
   d. put the pieces together

3. Which of these is **appropriate** for a dog?
   a. a tennis racket
   b. a library card
   c. a rubber ball
   d. a CD player

4. If we **scamper** in the park, we
   a. drag our feet and moan
   b. skip happily along
   c. ask directions
   d. sit on a bench

5. A **frail** person might
   a. give in to temptation
   b. win a lottery
   c. work for the railroad
   d. stand up for what is right

6. Which is a **symptom** of fear?
   a. giving a brave speech
   b. learning to ride a bike
   c. feeling your heart pound
   d. wearing a scary mask

7. How might a bride **adorn** her wedding gown?
   a. with fabric softener
   b. with pearls and lace
   c. with an apron
   d. with wedding cake

8. It is a **landslide** if you got
   a. 197 votes and I got 5
   b. 150 votes and I got 149
   c. as many votes as I did
   d. elected

9. Most of all, **hostages** want to be
   a. in charge of a party
   b. on vacation
   c. on television
   d. set free

10. If cattle **rampage**, you should
    a. take cover in a safe place
    b. take photographs
    c. sell tickets
    d. blow a whistle

11. A **colossal** tree is likely to be
    a. found in the desert
    b. short and bushy
    c. very tall and thick
    d. home to woodpeckers

12. Carmakers **warrant** that they
    a. always tell the truth
    b. will make repairs as needed
    c. will teach you to drive
    d. can search your car

Selecting Word Meanings

*For each of the following items circle the choice that is most nearly the **same** in meaning as the word in **boldface**.*

1. may **warrant** another visit
   a. refuse   b. justify   c. request   d. avoid

2. **adopt** a stray kitten
   a. walk   b. abandon   c. brush   d. take in

3. the **dominant** idea in the article
   a. main   b. silliest   c. only   d. missing

4. expect **courtesy** from the hotel staff
   a. gifts   b. rudeness   c. politeness   d. invitations

5. a **drab** scarf
   a. warm   b. long   c. dull   d. bright

6. too **frail** to travel
   a. frightened   b. sickly   c. busy   d. lazy

7. a **hazardous** mission
   a. dangerous   b. secret   c. delicate   d. pointless

8. **noticeable** changes in temperature
   a. uncomfortable   b. sudden   c. slight   d. obvious

9. a wild **rampage**
   a. frenzy   b. reaction   c. visit   d. dream

10. listened with **genuine** interest
    a. pretended   b. intense   c. sincere   d. amused

11. **huddle** by the dim candle
    a. sit   b. cluster   c. read   d. gossip

12. **attentive** to details
    a. indifferent   b. drawn   c. faithful   d. alert

For each item below study the **boldface** word in which there is a blank. If a letter is missing, fill in the blank to make a correctly spelled word. If the word is already spelled correctly, leave the blank empty.

1. a painful **s__mptom**

2. an absolute **nec__essity**

3. remarkable **generos__ty**

4. a **car__free** mood

5. **den__e** mist

6. **overth__ow** the leaders

7. a sports **ar__na**

8. an **a__ile** move

9. **analy__e** the situation

10. **as__emble** the tent

11. a **co__lossal** mess

12. a frightened **hosta__e**

Antonyms

For each of the following items circle the choice that is most nearly the **opposite** in meaning to the word in **boldface**.

1. **absolute** knowledge
   a. certain   b. faulty   c. special   d. limited

2. a new **ally**
   a. opponent   b. partner   c. relative   d. voter

3. **scamper** down the hill
   a. hop   b. roll   c. stroll   d. dash

4. **assist** the chef
   a. help   b. blame   c. watch   d. hamper

5. **adorn** the stage
   a. decorate   b. build   c. damage   d. remove

6. **compliment** her efforts
   a. criticize   b. applaud   c. measure   d. reward

7. a **fatal** blow
   a. harmless   b. painful   c. deadly   d. shocking

8. **mistrust** my friend
   a. doubt   b. question   c. avoid   d. believe

Words have been left out of the following passage. For each numbered item in the passage, fill in the circle next to the word in the margin that best fills the blank space. Then answer each question below by writing a sentence that contains one of the words you have chosen.

When the new mayor takes office, she will __1__ new people to fill jobs in city government. The mayor is expected to name new deputy mayors and commissioners. She might also choose someone to direct a special community outreach project.

1. ○ overthrow
   ○ appoint
   ○ assist
   ○ offend

The mayor must conduct a __2__ search for just the right people for the jobs. People who want to work for the mayor must have an interest in the city, strong speaking and writing skills, and a desire to serve the public.

2. ○ thorough
   ○ peculiar
   ○ carefree
   ○ hazardous

Before offering anyone a job, the mayor and her staff will discuss the __3__ of each candidate. For example, someone who has strong skills but does not get along well with others would be wrong for the job. And a well-liked person with a quick temper could also cause problems.

3. ○ symptoms
   ○ courtesies
   ○ merits
   ○ allies

The mayor will take the time to __4__ her choices carefully. She knows that she must find the best person for each position. And she knows that it is important for the public to respect her judgment. Most of all she needs a team that will serve the city well and make it a better place to live and work.

4. ○ regain
   ○ adopt
   ○ babble
   ○ analyze

5. What will the mayor do before she offers anyone a job?

_____

6. What must the mayor do to find the right people for the jobs?

_____

7. In what way will the new mayor affect jobs in city goverment?

_____

8. What will the mayor do to try to make wise choices?

_____

 **Analogies** *In each of the following circle the letter for the item that best completes the comparison. Then explain the relationship on the lines provided.*

1. **captivity** is to **freedom** as
    a. courtesy is to care
    b. fatal is to deadly
    c. noticeable is to obvious
    d. abstract is to real

    Relationship: _____

    _____

    _____

    _____

2. **appropriate** is to **seize** as
    a. overthrow is to support
    b. adopt is to reject
    c. scamper is to scurry
    d. merit is to failing

    Relationship: _____

    _____

    _____

3. **peculiar** is to **ordinary** as
    a. rampage is to riot
    b. assist is to hinder
    c. regain is to recover
    d. illegal is to criminal

    Relationship: _____

    _____

    _____

    _____

4. **compliment** is to **good** as
    a. praise is to bad
    b. blame is to good
    c. insult is to bad
    d. criticize is to good

    Relationship: _____

    _____

    _____

Challenge: Make up your own
Write a comparison using the words in the box below. (Hint: There are three possible analogies.) Then write the relationship on the lines provided.

sand	tiny	enemy	lawn
red	shape	beach	color
colossal	grass	triangle	ally

Analogy: _____ is to _____ as _____ is to _____.

Relationship: _____

_____

Word Families

*The words in **boldface** in the sentences below are related to words introduced in Units 13–16. For example, the adjectives ineffective and discourteous in item 1 are related to the adjective effective (Unit 16) and the noun courtesy (Unit 13). Based on your understanding of the unit words that follow, circle the related word in **boldface** that best completes each sentence.*

abstract	effective	captivity	frail	warrant
assist	attentive	agile	compliment	courtesy
deliberate	adorn	fatal	ally	illegal
manufacture	merit	mistrust	offend	analyze

1. This medicine is so old that is it totally (**ineffective/discourteous**).

2. The fiery train crash caused two (**fatalities/abstractions**).

3. The jury's (**deliberations/illegalities**) lasted for five days before a verdict was reached.

4. Regular stretching and exercise can help older people keep some of the (**agility/frailty**) they had when they were young.

5. The Swiss are famous as (**assistants/manufacturers**) of fine watches.

6. The speaker thanked the audience members for their (**attentiveness/ offensiveness**).

7. The rooms of the mansion were filled with elegant (**warranties/ adornments**).

8. Many family resorts provide (**complimentary/captive**) video games for their guests to enjoy.

9. The United States and Canada have a long-standing (**analysis/alliance**) as trading and defense partners.

10. Three police officers earned medals of honor for (**mistrustful/meritorious**) service to the community.

Use the clue and the given letters to complete each word. Write the missing letters of the word in the appropriate boxes. Then use the circled letters and the drawing to answer the CHALLENGE question below.

1. To make a gurgling sound

☐ ⃝ B B ⃝ ☐

2. Another verb that means "to recover or get back"

☐ E ☐ ☐ ⃝ N

3. Thickheaded

⃝ ☐ ☐ S ☐

4. Someone held prisoner

☐ O ⃝ ☐ ☐ G ⃝

5. Football players do this on the field

☐ U ⃝ ☐ ⃝ ☐

6. A field of interest, activity, conflict, or debate

☐ ☐ E ⃝ ☐

Challenge:

What caused this mess?

☐ ☐ ☐ ☐ ☐ ☐ ☐ ☐ ☐

Definitions

Choose the word from the box that matches each definition. Write the word on the line provided.

adorn	analyze	appoint	colossal	distress
dungeon	focus	generosity	heroic	manufacture
missionary	nourish	offend	peculiar	proceed
provision	quake	regain	toxic	unfit

1. a dark room or cell used as a prison, usually underground _____

2. to shake or move back and forth; to tremble _____

3. the quality of being charitable to others _____

4. to make something, especially using machinery _____

5. not physically or mentally healthy _____

6. to feed or help grow and develop; to support _____

7. to cause hurt feelings, anger, or injury _____

8. brave, noble, or larger than life _____

9. to go on or continue; to start again after a pause _____

10. to study carefully or in detail _____

11. a step taken ahead of time; a condition, as in a contract _____

12. odd or curious; not like the normal or usual _____

13. poisonous or deadly _____

14. deep worry or suffering; being in danger or trouble _____

15. amazingly large, great, or powerful _____

Antonyms

Choose the word from the box that is most nearly **opposite** in meaning to each group of words. Write the word on the line provided.

1. ordinary, regular, usual, average _____

2. to criticize, insult, denounce _____

3. gentle, refined, polite _____

4. freshwater, land _____

5. smooth, even, regular _____

6. to reject, disown, abandon _____

7. a penalty, deduction, fine _____

8. to scatter, break up, disperse _____

9. faith, hope, trust, confidence _____

10. actual, real, physical, concrete _____

11. to acquit, free, release _____

12. alert, clever, smart _____

13. overlooked, hidden, obscure _____

14. insincere, trivial, frivolous, foolish _____

15. to disgrace, demote, lower _____

16. an option, extra, luxury _____

17. freedom, independence, liberty _____

18. to lumber, lag, dawdle, stroll _____

19. early, prompt, on time _____

20. to parch, dry _____

abstract

adopt

assemble

bonus

captivity

coarse

compliment

convict

dense

despair

drench

earnest

elevate

fatal

jagged

marine

necessity

noticeable

outstanding

register

scamper

site

tardy

variety

warrant

Completing the Sentence

Choose the word from the box that best completes each sentence below. Write the word in the space provided.

Group A

discard	extraordinary	grumble	inspire
pointless	sift	spree	uneasy

1. My dad may _____ about it, but he always walks our dog at night.

2. Many people feel _____ about traveling in stormy weather.

3. It took hours for my mom to _____ through that big pile of old magazines, but she enjoyed the task.

4. She found a(n) _____ number of magazines with stories about the rich and the famous.

5. By the end of the afternoon, Mom decided to _____ all but two of the magazines.

Group B

absolute	ally	genuine	huddle
illegal	landslides	overthrow	symptom

1. Public protests have led to the _____ of cruel and corrupt rulers throughout history.

2. In many cases people were outraged that their rulers made _____ use of tax money to buy luxuries while many citizens lived in poverty.

3. Rebels have refused to allow such rulers to continue to have _____ control over all areas of people's lives.

4. When free elections have been held, representatives of the people have won by overwhelming _____.

5. Such democratic victories have given people _____ opportunities to lead better lives.

Classifying

Choose the word from the box that goes best with each group of words. Write the word in the space provided. Then explain what the words have in common.

arena	bristle	chant	circular	drab
juvenile	mistrust	reflect	site	treaty

1. beige, tan, gray, _____

_____

2. whisker, spine, quill, _____

_____

3. carol, hymn, _____

_____

4. infant, _____, adult

_____

5. _____, reflection, reflective, reflector

_____

6. leaflet, pamphlet, flyer, advertisement, _____

_____

7. stadium, auditorium, _____, theater

_____

8. sight, _____, cite

_____

9. pact, accord, _____

_____

10. misfit, misprint, mislead, _____

_____

FINAL MASTERY TEST

 **Definitions** *For each item choose the word that matches the definition. Then write the word on the line provided.*

1. to close off or keep people or supplies from going in or out
   a. dungeon   b. enclose   c. grasp   d. blockade   _____

2. changing little by little
   a. gradual   b. jagged   c. unfit   d. agile   _____

3. lack of sameness; a category of plants or animals
   a. spree   b. variety   c. mission   d. extreme   _____

4. to unite or join for a special purpose
   a. adorn   b. adopt   c. ally   d. assist   _____

5. to guide, excite, uplift, or encourage
   a. inspire   b. focus   c. magnify   d. reflect   _____

6. done or said on purpose; at a slow or steady pace
   a. thorough   b. hazardous   c. dense   d. deliberate   _____

7. a quality that deserves reward or praise
   a. mistrust   b. merit   c. symptom   d. haste   _____

8. to take over or use as one's own, often without permission
   a. compliment b. warrant   c. appropriate d. sift   _____

9. in great supply, easily available; more than enough
   a. alert   b. awkward   c. plentiful   d. tidy   _____

10. a widespread outbreak of disease; sudden rapid growth
    a. epidemic   b. ancestor   c. noble   d. policy   _____

11. to draw attention to something else; to confuse or disturb
    a. blossom   b. distract   c. dismiss   d. survive   _____

12. to set up, start, organize, or bring about; to prove beyond doubt
    a. appoint   b. assemble   c. rampage   d. establish   _____

13. beginning or first

 a. annual   b. sturdy   c. urgent   d. initial   _____

14. a load; something that is very hard to bear

 a. pledge   b. sponsor   c. burden   d. stampede   _____

15. not used, filled, or lived in; without thought or expression

 a. vacant   b. suitable   c. content   d. foul   _____

16. honest and truthful

 a. gallant   b. sincere   c. weary   d. abstract   _____

17. having no meaning or effect

 a. tardy   b. pointless   c. uneasy   d. dominant   _____

18. to get back; to reach again

 a. overthrow   b. nourish   c. provision   d. regain   _____

19. a lively or wild outburst of activity

 a. spree   b. chant   c. juvenile   d. treaty   _____

20. a major product, material, part, or item regularly used

 a. ration   b. drought   c. staple   d. routine   _____

 Part of Speech   *For each item below indicate the part of speech of the word in* **boldface.** *In the space provided write* N *for noun,* V *for verb, or* A *for adjective.*

21. _____ **discipline** the puppy

22. _____ the election **register**

23. _____ **lance** the infection

24. _____ **troublesome** tasks

25. _____ **attentive** to my wishes

26. _____ join the **huddle**

27. _____ **babble** on for hours

28. _____ **effective** on insect bites

29. _____ a generous **portion**

30. _____ **trudge** home from work

**Completing the Sentence**

Choose the word from the box that best completes each sentence. Write the word in the space provided. (You may have to change the word's ending.)

Group A

appoint	carefree	collide	enclose
extend	feeble	magnify	response

31. My aunt wears special glasses that can _____ small print.

32. Don't forget to _____ a gift card inside the box so that the bride will know who sent her the present.

33. The President will _____ ambassadors and members of the cabinet.

34. It is always a treat to find that you have a _____ afternoon ahead of you with no chores or homework to do.

Group B

adorn	clatter	demonstrate	dominant
employ	toxic	sensible	sponsor

35. Blue, green, and purple are the _____ colors in my wardrobe.

36. Even a small amount of shellfish can be _____ to someone who is very allergic to it.

37. For our Fourth of July picnic, we will _____ the tables and the yard with flags and red, white, and blue flowers.

38. The _____ of our soccer team donated money for uniforms, equipment, and trophies.

*Circle the letter next to the word or expression that best completes the sentence or answers the question. Pay special attention to the word in **boldface**.*

39. A family might **dwell** in
   a. an apartment
   b. a teakettle
   c. a magazine
   d. a videotape

40. It is a **courtesy** to
   a. make fun of me
   b. finish my dessert
   c. climb my ladder
   d. open a door for me

41. A **frail** person is
   a. strong
   b. weak
   c. wise
   d. jumpy

42. In **extreme** heat, I might
   a. turn on the furnace
   b. eat a heavy meal
   c. wear light clothing
   d. clean out the attic

43. Which is a **disaster**?
   a. the hiccups
   b. an earthquake
   c. a rainbow
   d. a book report

44. To **lash** signs to a fence,
   a. use rope
   b. use glue
   c. use water
   d. use paint

45. A **scholar** does a lot of
   a. singing
   b. skating
   c. studying
   d. spying

46. To plan an **ambush**, find a
   a. good book
   b. flowerpot
   c. tall chair
   d. hiding spot

47. A sore toe might **indicate**
   a. an infection
   b. nail polish
   c. comfortable shoes
   d. new socks

48. Many **hazardous** tools are
   a. flat
   b. new
   c. sharp
   d. squishy

49. Most people **recall**
   a. a recipe for pumpkin pie
   b. their own birthday
   c. all the state capitals
   d. how to play polo

50. To do a **thorough** cleaning,
   a. be sure to wash the dishes
   b. be sure to paint the doors
   c. be sure to sweep the halls
   d. be sure to scrub everything

INDEX

The following is a list of all the words taught in the units of this book. The number after each entry indicates the page on which the word is first introduced, but the word also appears in exercises on later pages.